**SOMERSET MUSIC
EDUCATION PROGRAMME**

Growing with music:
Key Stage 2

Teacher's Book B

Michael Stocks and Andrew Maddocks

LONGMAN

Acknowledgements

The Somerset Music Education Programme started because many local primary teachers and Heads believed in the educational benefits to be gained from including music within the day to day curriculum of the primary school – and were prepared to give time and effort to the improvement of their own music and teaching skills. As a result, through singing and aural activity reinforced by movement and instrumental work, many children in Somerset primary schools have grown in musical confidence and awareness. It has been an evolutionary process in which we have learned from each other.

We should have made little progress if we had not also tried to benefit from the experience of distinguished music teachers and writers on music education from previous generations: to mention a few, we wish to acknowledge our debt to the work and writings of John Curwen; to the collections and observations of Cecil Sharp and Percy Grainger; to Bernarr Rainbow's research into the history of music education in Britain; and to Zoltán Kodály. The Somerset project owes much to the music education practice in Hungary which grew out of Kodály's insight and leadership and the work of his students and disciples, so many of whom are now distinguished teachers and music educators of international standing and influence. To our Hungarian friends in particular, therefore, and to those many acquaintances in North America who share our admiration of the Hungarian example – our grateful thanks.

Finally, we should like to acknowledge our gratitude to the Winston Churchill Memorial Trust for making possible study visits to Hungary and the United States of America, and to the contribution of the Calouste Gulbenkian Foundation, without whose support (along with that of Somerset County Council) the preparation of draft materials, their trials in Somerset schools and their dissemination beyond Somerset would not have been possible.

Michael Stocks   **Andrew Maddocks**
Adviser for Music   Advisory Teacher for Music

(Somerset Education Department)

Contents

Preface

Somerset Music Education Programme: its purpose and context

The Somerset Music Education Programme (SMEP) aims to develop the musicianship of children across the whole of the primary age range by increasing aural awareness, encouraging 'inner ear' response and enabling musical thinking. It is concerned with those elements of music which are common to most musical styles.

Key Stage 1 and Key Stage 2A are the result of well-tried practice in Somerset primary schools. Key Stage 2B (for Years 5 and 6) is based upon this experience and is an extension to Key Stage 2A.

The Programme is not a method, but offers to the teacher a structure upon which a music curriculum can be based; it also contains a sequence of skills and concepts designed to facilitate a process of learning which has progression and purpose. At Key Stage 2B, instruments feature more strongly – particularly when fixed pitch concepts have been introduced – because performance on instruments requires knowledge of fixed pitch rather than relative pitch.

As with other areas of the school curriculum, a music curriculum is required to have breadth, balance, coherence and relevance. This can only be achieved if the teacher builds his/her own scheme of work within the curriculum plan of the whole school. The Somerset Music Education Programme is designed to help teachers achieve this, with room to incorporate local needs and individual teaching strengths – and to support the teacher in meeting the requirements of the National Curriculum.

Somerset Music Education Programme: the components

Stage 1

Teacher's Book 1	0 582 03937 1
Cassette 1	0 582 03936 3
The Stage 1 Evaluation Pack (Teacher's Book and Cassette)	0 582 09750 9

Stage 2A

Teacher's Book 2A	0 582 03944 4
Cassette 2A	0 582 03942 8
Pupil's Book 1	0 582 03947 9
Pupil's Book 2	0 582 03946 0
The Stage 2A Evaluation Pack (Teacher's Book 2A; Pupil's Books 1 & 2; Cassette 2A)	0 582 09751 7

Stage 2B

Teacher's Book 2B	0 582 03943 6
Cassette 2B	0 582 03941 X
Pupil's Book 3	0 582 03945 2
Pupil's Book 4	0 582 03948 7
The Stage 2B Evaluation Pack (Teacher's Book 2B; Pupil's Books 3 & 4; Cassette 2B)	0 582 09752 5

There are separate Assessment Sheets provided as copymasters at the end of the Teacher's Books to cover the requirements of the National Curriculum for England, Scotland, Wales and Northern Ireland.

Introduction

Somerset Music Education Programme and the school curriculum

So many teachers and parents value music for the contribution it makes to the life and ethos of the school. Most primary teachers are well-disposed towards music and acknowledge the significance of its inclusion as a foundation subject of the National Curriculum. It is now generally recognised that music is a statutory entitlement in the curriculum structure.

However, it is also generally recognised that the number of teachers in the primary sector who have had an opportunity to include music as a part of their initial training are few and that opportunities for in-service training in curriculum music have been limited. But music can no longer be put away on the shelf; it has ceased to be an area of the curriculum to be left to the so-called 'specialist' (if they ever existed). It is now a requirement that music be taught to all pupils aged 5 to 14. So it is not surprising that large numbers of primary teachers are apprehensive about the prospect of including music within their school curriculum plan – an understandable reaction in view of the strong implicit messages which have been communicated over so many years by so many of the 'musically skilled'. Long may the musical 'high flyers' flourish, for they give so much pleasure; but the music curriculum in our schools must now turn its attention to *all* children, rather than the gifted few.

In the secondary phase, developments in GCSE have already led the way. What we now need is an approach to the music curriculum which is governed by the needs of children in the primary phase and which sets new targets for music in the secondary school. This is what *Growing with Music* sets out to help achieve.

Growing with Music is a programme which helps to make music accessible to teachers, particularly those without previous training. Most of all, as a programme in line with National Curriculum requirements, it offers to our children a chance to realise their musical potential, self-esteem and independence (see page 76).

The programme is mainly concerned with helping the pupil acquire those music skills and concepts which are basic to music-making activity and which are common to many musical styles. As a result, the pupil develops his/her musical ability and finds that the music of other countries and historical periods becomes more accessible. The ingredients of style become recognisable and more easily understood because the student acquires the musical experience and knowledge needed to appraise and to evaluate what he/she hears.

Melodies from the following countries appear in the Programme:

Belgium	Holland	Russia
Canada	Hungary	Scotland
Czechoslovakia	India	Serbia
Denmark	Ireland	Sweden
England	Israel	Trinidad
France	Jamaica	Ukraine
Germany	Liberia	USA
Ghana	Philippines	Virgin Islands
Greece	Poland	Wales
Guyana	Polynesia	

The Somerset Music Education Programme comprises the following material:

GROWING WITH MUSIC: KEY STAGE 1
(Infants: age 4–7 years)
This stage suggests ideas for increasing the musical awareness of younger children by listening, singing, movement and playing.

GROWING WITH MUSIC: KEY STAGE 2A
(Lower Junior: age 7–9 years)
Intended for junior 'starters', this is also a continuation programme for those who began with *Growing with Music: Key Stage 1*. The repertoire is chosen for this age-range, and written material is included for the children to use.

GROWING WITH MUSIC: KEY STAGE 2B
(Upper Junior: age 9–11 years)
This is a continuation programme for those seeking to move on from *Growing with Music: Key Stage 2A*.

Preparing for Key Stage 2B

When your children are ready to start Key Stage 2B it is likely that they will have completed Key Stage 2A and that, depending upon the class and the teacher, this will have taken approximately two years. For children who have not worked with this programme before, it is recommended that time is spent with Key Stage 2A before embarking on Key Stage 2B.

Key Stage 2A will have helped the children:
  (i) to acquire a range of basic skills,
  (ii) to use their skills in developing essential music concepts,
  (iii) to grow in confidence with voice and instruments.

They will have acquired a large repertoire of song material and will have reached a stage of aural awareness which equips them well for reading and writing music notation. Working with music spontaneously, as well as with notation, the children will have composed short melodies and will have an understanding of their structure.

Key Stage 2B is aimed at the upper junior age-range. As with Key Stage 2A, there are a teacher's book and two pupil's books, but the programme moves more quickly and assumptions are made to take account of Key Stage 2A experience. The teacher's book sets out to be supportive in such a way that the teacher without initial training in music is helped to be aware of the learning process at each point in the programme. Without doubt, in-service training in these circumstances remains invaluable.

The *Teacher's Book 2B* contains a Song collection, and Copymasters which offer extra musical material for the children to use. In addition to an interesting repertoire of vocal melody, the Copymasters include melodic material for instruments, music for instrumental ensemble and choral music (suitable for reading as well as for rote teaching). All reading material is carefully structured so that, most of the time, the children are asked to read according to previous aural experience. The melodic material is taken from many different parts of the world, but a central focus for selection has been the indigenous repertoire of the British Isles.

About the Course programme (Key Stage 2B)

The Skill/Concept index (page 17) is the structural backbone for the course and the Course programme suggests ways in which 'flesh and muscles' might be added. Many primary teachers will already be aware that education (music, or otherwise) can never be a matter of simply teaching items from a list or following a 'method'. For music education to take place there is no substitute for the teacher bringing his/her own imagination into the process so that the child's musical experience and progression has a context of, or relationship to, other experience. The Song collection is an important resource; it includes vocal melody of quality from many countries and in many styles.

The Teacher's Book is largely concerned with **music activities**, so that the child comes to recognise and acknowledge music as a rewarding and pleasurable activity – rather than a means of merely interpreting notation and symbols. **Extension activities** are offered, partly to suggest activities beyond the classroom, and partly for those children with a capability to undertake more advanced work. Musical examples are provided in the Teacher's Book text, to assist teachers in their teaching, e.g. on the board. These are labelled **U1–U81** (pages 19–99).

The Pupil's Books 3 and 4 cannot offer musical sound; because they are a printed medium, they tend to be concerned with the notational aspects of music education. It is for the teacher to ensure that whenever the children are working with notation (an essential ingredient in music education), they are doing so from a position of aural understanding and confidence. The music activity normally precedes the use of the Pupil's Books, in such a way that the children are ready to cope with the musical thinking demanded and are able to work individually and with others in a defined direction and to a clear purpose.

The Pupil's Books, therefore, provide an opportunity for the children to consolidate and extend their music experience – at Key Stage 2B, with increasing independence of the teacher. The children are encouraged to apply their music experience and newly acquired skills in different contexts or new situations. Partners and group work provide mutual support and an opportunity for working in parts – one of the most satisfying and motivating features of music-making.

The Key Stage 2B materials

The *Growing with Music* teaching materials for use with Years 5 and 6 consist of the following items:

1 TEACHER'S BOOK B
See the section below for details of the support material available in this book.

2 SONG COLLECTION ON CASSETTE
As well as the Song collection, the Choral files and Orchestral (see pages 197–247 of this Teacher's Book) are included on the accompanying cassette.

3 PUPIL'S BOOK 3 and **PUPIL'S BOOK 4**

Support materials

At the back of the Teacher's Book are many pages (162–270) which the teacher may photocopy for distribution to individuals or the class as a whole. These Copymasters contain a variety of material which has been prepared with particular needs in mind. Precise reference is made to each of these in the Teacher's Book, and occasionally in the Pupil's Book (see the front of each book). They should be used at the discretion of the teacher, according to individual need and local circumstance. These photocopies can accumulate in pupils' own files and could contribute significantly to a record of achievement for individual pupil's profile.

- **Additional melodic material**
  These include: reading sheets (songs, two-part reading material), extension material and games.

- **Choral file**
  Precise reference is made to each of these choral pieces in the Teacher's Book. They are specially prepared in two or three parts. Apart from some of the later examples, they match the reading ability of the pupil at that stage of the Programme. In line with convention, choral file music is read from the vocal score.

- **Orchestral file**
  Precise reference is made to each of these instrumental ensemble pieces in the Teacher's Book. Apart from some of the later examples, one of the parts always matches the reading ability of the pupil at that stage of the Programme. Some parts often require more experienced instrumentalists, and therefore help cater for the differentiation of ability which will naturally occur in most classes. In line with convention, orchestral file music is read from separate parts.

- **Playscript**
  It will be useful for the teacher to be able to photocopy a number of scripts for the play 'The Ugsome Thing' (Pupil's Book 3), particularly if the pupils are preparing a music score, or are involved in the production arrangements.

- **Writing sheets**
  Pupils should be discouraged from writing in the Pupil's Books. The writing sheets provide all the formats the pupils will require and can be collected in the pupils' own files as a record of written work done.

- **Teacher Lesson Planning Sheet**
  This provides the teacher with a way of setting out the information he/she needs to plan an effective music session.

Using the Pupil's Books in your teaching

The Pupil's Books are an important resource for child-centred activity. They should be considered as an integral part of your teaching. Pupil's Books 3 and 4 provide opportunities for children to work individually and, quite often, with a partner. In various ways, the tasks proposed will require the child to apply his/her developing aural, improvising, reading, writing and composing skills. However, the progress of the children is likely to be enhanced if they are presented with the pupil's book tasks only when there has been adequate listening and performing preparation in class.

The Pupil's Books enable a child to show his/her individual understanding, level of skill and musical achievement. A child's handling of the tasks will inform the teacher about the child's current learning situation and will suggest particular ways to further his/her progress. Similarly, the way in which the class as a whole responds to the tasks will inform the teacher's planning; the record of assessment sheets (pages 255–270) will also make an essential contribution to this.

Teachers are aware that in different areas of the curriculum children develop individually and at varying rates. A widening range of achievement in music will become evident as time passes. This will require the teacher to be increasingly aware of the varying needs of the children and to be constantly examining the role which the Pupil's Books have in the children's learning process. For example, it is quite possible that some children would benefit from pursuing a task beyond the ideas suggested on the page; others, however, may need to be guided into approaching the task in a more limited way. In other words, the teacher needs to have a menu of further ideas to help meet the requirements of differentiation. The extension activities in the Teacher's Book may be a useful resource for this purpose.

Using voice and instrument in music education

There are two performing media for music – voice and instrument. In music education, the distinction between the two is significant (see Key Stage 2 Teacher's Book A).

In this course, particularly with the introduction of fixed pitch concepts, instruments feature more strongly than at Key Stage 2A. The children are asked frequently to transfer their vocal performance to an instrument and, from the latter part of Pupil's Book 3, are encouraged to play instruments from reading fixed pitch staff notation. Not only is their aural/vocal experience reinforced by these activities with instruments, but also the opportunity is created for performing in instrumental ensembles at a level, and with material, appropriate to the child's level of skill and musical understanding (see orchestral file *Copymasters*). Thus, personal confidence grows and musical competence increases.

The teacher must always remember that an ability to read from written notation should never be presented as a more desirable activity than making music with pleasure and understanding in an active and spontaneous fashion. In music education, the spontaneous tradition in music needs to feature on equal terms with the interpretive written tradition.

The place of music in everyday life

Few people give thought to the part that music plays in their lives. In fact, music appears more commonly than we recognise and is often influential in the way it affects our attitudes and decision-making – whether it be wallpaper music in the workshop, 'soft sell' music in the supermarket or 'memory jogging' music in advertising media. It could be said that no generation in history has ever heard so much music, in such a wide range of styles and with such intensity of purpose.

Music in education must obviously take account of this and ensure that programmes of study take every opportunity to relate music education in class to the place of music in the world outside.

Some of the pages in Pupil's Books 3 and 4 are labelled MUSIC IN OUR LIVES. These pages are particularly angled to the outside world of music, and other pages in which the children have been invited to compose might be used equally to this purpose. Composing has more meaning and relevance if it is done for a reason. As with language composition, composing in music usually takes place with a particular audience or occasion in mind; but music composers must also remember that their work is brought to life only through performing. The teacher should therefore be looking for good opportunities to bring music to life in this way. Indeed, the primary school is an ideal environment for this, particularly since so much primary education takes place through theme and topic work.

Composing in Pupil's Book 3

If all composing invitations in Pupil's Book 3 are accepted, the list looks as follows:

Page	
7	A new day (hymn)
13	Magic and spells (goblin song)
14	The cruel giant
17	Haunted house
18	Lullaby
24	Summers past and to come
25	The cheerful old woman
33	Folk dance
38	Fanfares
40	Making a climax
42	Passing notes (1) (lullaby)
46	A supporters' song
48	A building song

These compositions might be used as follows:

	Item	Pupil's Book 3 pages
A	Play: 'The Ugsome Thing' (A play for upper juniors to perform to younger children, aged 5–7: script in Copymasters, p. 250–4)	14, 25, 40, 48 (These songs can be used directly with the script)
B	Make up own play, using a selection of compositions	(e.g.) 7, 18, 24, 40, 42
C	Folk dancing, using tunes composed by the children	31, 33
D	Improvised drama	(e.g.) 5, 6, 13, 15, 17, 23, 30, 37, 38, 40
E	For use in the life of the school	7, 24, 37, 38, 46
F	School fête	24, 30, 31, 33, 38, 46

Composing in Pupil's Book 4

If all composing invitations in Pupil's Book 4 are accepted, the list looks as follows:

Page 11   A Slovakian dance
      13   March for a grand occasion
      23   Games galore
      24   Beachcombers
      27   Composing an alphabet song
      31   A welcome song
      32   Caribbean rhythm
      43   A donkey song
      44   Musical clocks
      47   . . . strings attached (puppet show theme tune)

These compositions might be used as follows:

	Item	Pupil's Book 4 pages
A	Puppet show	11, 27, 31, 43, 44, 47
B	Make up own play, using a selection of compositions	13, 23, 27, 31, 43
C	Folk dancing, using tunes composed by the children	9, 10, 11, 25, 34, 35
D	Improvised drama	(e.g.) 1, 3, 7, 12, 27, 31, 44
E	For use in the life of the school	13, 23, 24, 27, 31, 43
F	Special occasion	11, 13, 31, 32, 44

Compositions of this kind need to feature also in school concerts and presentations. It is for the teacher to decide how this work can be used to greatest effect so that the children's achievements are seen to be valued.

Rather than being confined to specially prepared music presented by the chosen few, school concerts and presentations to parents should also be seen as an opportunity to present the work which has been done in class by all the children – as with art, or cookery.

Assessment of the music curriculum

Recent curriculum reform in all countries of the United Kingdom requires that assessment is an integral part of the educational process – by informing curriculum planning, by making possible the recording of individual pupil progress and by supporting the evaluation of teaching performance. The outcomes of these reforms are expressed in different ways for England, Northern Ireland, Scotland and Wales because each country has reviewed the curriculum within its own context and terms of reference. The result is a rich tapestry of experience which makes rewarding reading for all teachers. The 'Growing with Music' programme relates strongly to the music curriculum objectives expressed in each of the four countries, as shown in the Appendix to this book which contains charts connecting 'Growing with Music' to each country's Programmes of Study.

Assessment has been an integral part of the preparation of the 'Growing with Music' programme. The Skill/Concept index (page 17) is in itself a powerful support for assessment, but probably too detailed for most teachers to use as a basis for reasonable assessment procedures. Consequently, Record of Assessment sheets are provided at the end of this Teacher's Book (see *Copymasters*, pages 255–270) for schools in England, Northern Ireland, Scotland and Wales. These sheets contain statutory statements (end of Key Stage or Levels, according to the country) and interim statements in line with Attainment Target strands. The teacher should use those sheets which correspond to the level of the class. It is for the teacher to decide, in accordance with his/her assessment practice in other curriculum areas or with assessment systems already in place in the school, whether the assessment criteria columns should contain a tick, or a felt-tipped pen colour-coded mark, a graded mark or a reference to a written descriptive judgement elsewhere.

Music Curriculum Assessment (England)

National Curriculum documentation makes it clear that assessment arrangements for music will not include nationally prescribed tests and, in consequence, concludes that assessment of achievement in music will for most pupils be by teachers only. It further recommends that assessment be made against the End of Key Stage Statements. It also says that assessment should be simple and part of the classroom process, thus making only reasonable demands on time.

In this programme two assessments are proposed for Key Stage 1, and four assessments for Key Stage 2 – an annual record of pupil progress by criterion statements under the two attainment targets of Performing/Composing and Listening/Appraising.

Record of Assessment sheets for Key Stage 2 (England) are provided as Copymasters (pages 255–258). The 'Name' column is for the names of the pupils to be listed. The 'Comments' column is for the teacher to make observations about individual pupils, particularly to inform reports to parents. The narrow columns in the middle relate to the assessment criteria which appear under the Attainment Targets Performing/Composing and Listening/Appraising.

Music Curriculum Assessment (Northern Ireland)

The Northern Ireland Curriculum: Music states that 'as music will not be the subject of compulsory assessment the statements of attainment contained in the document are included for the guidance of teachers only . . . (they) do not form part of the statutory provisions.'

The Record of Assessment sheets in this Programme relate to Levels 1–5, resulting in a record of pupil progress by statements of attainment under the two Attainment Targets of 'Making Music' and 'Responding to Music with understanding'. Although non-statutory they are a very useful guide to assessment criteria.

Record of Assessment sheets for Levels 2–5 (Northern Ireland) are provided as Copymasters (pages 259–262). The 'Name' column is for the names of the pupils to be listed. The 'Comments' column is for the teacher to make observations about individual pupils, particularly to inform reports to parents. The narrow columns in the middle relate to the statements of attainment which appear under the Attainment Targets.

Music Curriculum Assessment (Scotland)

Record of Assessment sheets for Levels B–D (Scotland) are provided as Copymasters (pages 263–266) at the end of this Teacher's Book. The 'Name' column is for the names of the pupils to be listed. The 'Comments' column is for the teacher to make observations about individual pupils, particularly to inform reports to parents. The narrow columns in the middle are aligned to the assessment criteria which relate to the Attainment Targets within the three common outcomes. The assessment criteria are 'concerned with pupils' abilities to:

- select, control and use media, technique, skills etc. appropriate to the task;
- generate, investigate and communicate their own ideas and show that they can develop and sustain them in a variety of ways;
- describe significant features of their own and others' work and make informed judgements and choices.'

The Record of Assessment sheets assume an annual assessment. The sheets labelled 'First Assessment' contain assessment criteria related to the 'Growing with Music' Programme which are also in line with the Attainment Targets. Sheets labelled 'Attainment Targets' are the final sheets at each Level. The full text of each attainment target is to be found in *Expressive Arts 5–14*.

Music Curriculum Assessment (Wales)

National Curriculum documentation makes it clear that assessment arrangements for music will not include nationally prescribed tests and, in consequence, concludes that assessments of achievement in music will for most pupils be by teachers only. It further recommends that assessments be made against the End of Stage Statements. It also says that assessment should be simple and part of the classroom process, thus making only reasonable demands on time.

In this programme two assessments are proposed for Key Stage 1, and four assessments for Key Stage 2 – an annual record of pupil progress by criterion statements under the three attainment targets of Performing, Composing and Appraising.

Record of Assessment sheets for Key Stage 2 (Wales) are provided as Copymasters (pages 267–270) at the end of this Teacher's Book. The 'Name' column is for the names of the pupils to be listed. The 'Comments' column is for the teacher to make observations about individual pupils, particularly to inform reports to parents. The narrow columns in the middle relate to the assessment criteria which appear under the Attainment Targets 'Performing, Composing and Appraising'.

'Growing with Music' in relation to music curricula

Details of the links between the 'Growing with Music' programme and the music curriculum criteria in England, Northern Ireland, Scotland and Wales are shown in the Appendix (pages 275–282).

Teacher's Book 1 contains Record of Assessment sheets and details of the music curriculum links at Key Stage 1 (England, Northern Ireland and Wales) and Level A (Scotland).

Course programme

- The aim of the *Course programme* is to provide for the teacher a skeletal structure upon which the flesh of living musical experience can be assembled. The content of the *Course programme* needs to be placed within an imaginative context, for it is in this way that the teaching takes on the vitality necessary for children successfully to acquire musical skills and concepts. So, although the teacher is aware of the chain of musical events that he/she wishes to pursue, his/her preparation should ensure a presentation which is dramatic, descriptive and imaginative.

- Hence, games and imaginary situations are a means for experiencing, discovering and learning. A theme such as 'A Journey' or 'Sharing' can provide an imaginative link for a sequence of musical events concerned with, for example, developing an awareness of phrase length. The teaching should always strive to be imaginative and musical.

Objective summary of *Growing with Music: Key Stage 2B*

Voice
To develop a basic understanding of voice technique. To develop intonation. To develop an ability to sing in parts.

Ear
To develop an ability to connect internalised musical thinking with vocal and instrumental performance, and with the composing and analysing processes.

Instruments
To develop a facility in playing melodic instruments and untuned percussion. To use instruments as a regular feature of class work. To maintain a part in a piece for instrumental ensemble.

Structure
To give experience of performing and composing with simple and extended structures. To work with canon. To use repetition, sequence, and climax when composing. To create an awareness of the role of tonality in structure. To introduce *Da Capo al Fine* and FIRST and SECOND time bars.

Rhythm
To introduce the whole note (𝅝), tied notes, sixteenth notes (♫♫), delayed notes (dotted notes) in simple time and compound time, passing notes, syncopation, the anacrusis, and the half-bar entry.

Pitch
To include the use of low lah, low soh, and te in solfa. To work with the upper and lower parts of the pentatone, the pentachord and hexachord on doh and lah, fixed pitch, the Natural Minor, and the Authentic and Plagal Major scales. To introduce tonality.

Literacy
To read and write melody and two-part music using staff and rhythm-solfa notations. To introduce the ¾ time signature, treble clef, and fixed pitch names. To read and write music in several styles.

Skill/Concept index

- *The Skill/Concept index* in the *Course programme* should be used in the knowledge that it is based on logical and musical principles, but that the order should not be adhered to rigidly if practical teaching sense suggests some deviation.

- Teachers should also be aware of the need to review established skills and concepts regularly, so as to exercise the memory, deepen understanding and extend ability still further.

- Although, at a given moment in time, the teaching plan is likely to be preoccupied with particular skills and concepts, overall the outcome for the child should be one of musical achievements – the result of a continuing encounter with fundamentals such as phrase, pulse, rhythm, pitch, dynamics, timbre, and an accumulation of experience, skills and knowledge.

The course

Skill/Concept

1 Reading in two parts from staff notation

▷ The children's previous experiences of working with two-part rhythm-solfa and reading single staff notation will have been good preparation for the two-part staff notation reading.

Music activities

KEY ▶

1 a Arrange the children into two convenient groups. Using the doh tetratone (**s–m–r–d**), establish the tone-set with the children through singing and handsigns. Designate a separate hand for each group and improvise two-part handsigns, such as **U1**–**U2**, so that each group reads and sings alternately. Let the second and succeeding phrases start on the last note of the previous phrase.

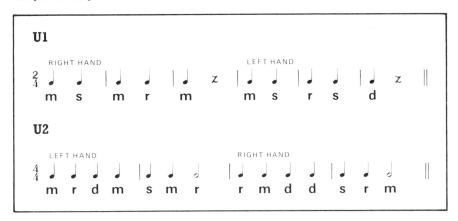

1 b Working with a partner, and using the notes of the doh pentatone, the first child improvises a melodic phrase (A), singing to solfa. The partner improvises a tapped rhythm second phrase (B). With alternating melodic and rhythmic phrases, the children structure an improvised piece with an A B A C format. The children should decide how long the phrases are to be before they start. Alternatively, they might perform first and afterwards discuss the length of the phrases used

1 c ☆ Pupil's Book 3, pages 1 and 2

EXTENSION ▶

1 d Ask individual children to improvise doh pentatonic phrases to form an A B A structure using 4-beat phrases, then using phrases of 8 or 6 beats. Each new phrase should begin on the last note of the previous phrase.

Skill/Concept

2 | Working in two parts

▷ The doh hexachord was introduced in Key Stage 2A. Teachers may wish to review the children's aural understanding of the doh hexachord before starting this section.

Music activities

KEY ▶

2 | a Establish the pitch relationships by singing **d–r–m–f–s–l–s–f–m–r–d** with handsigns, which the children then repeat. The teacher now shows a series of melodic phrases with handsigns (see **U3–U4** for examples) which the children repeat; individual children should be invited to lead the class. Occasionally, change the working pitch.

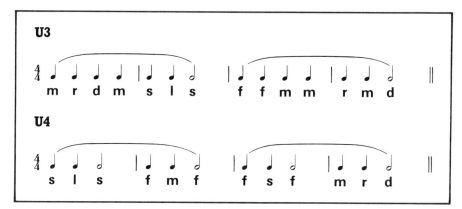

2 | b Invite a child to show an improvised melodic phrase with handsigns (using a doh hexachord) which the class sings. Ask the child to conclude the phrase with a two-note chord shown by two simultaneous handsigns, sung by two groups of the class.

2 | c Sing a series of improvised melodic phrases to two class groups in turn, who repeat each phrase by tapping the rhythm only, and simultaneous with the next phrase, thus:

Teacher	Group 1	Group 2
Melodic phrase A Melodic phrase B Melodic phrase C Melodic phrase D *etc.*	———— Tapped phrase A ———— Tapped phrase C	———— ———— Tapped phrase B ————

☆ **Pupil's Book 3,**
pages 3 and 4

2 | **d**   Page 3: when the children in pairs have had sufficient time with the two pieces on this page, it is suggested that the class together should perform both two-part pieces.

Page 4: with these pieces, try to ensure that the reading is accurate as they work in pairs. When a pair is performing well, invite them to perform for the class. It may be helpful for some children first to tap the rhythm only as a preliminary to performing.

> Reading in two parts should begin to be a regular feature within the teaching. The examples in the Pupil's Books and the Reading Sheets can be returned to frequently for further practice. Do not underestimate the value of repeating known examples; some might even be memorised – to the great advantage of the children. The teacher is advised:
>
> **(i)** in advance, to make the children aware of any potential difficulties in the exercise;
>
> **(ii)** to take one part at a time – first considering the rhythm, then the pitch;
>
> **(iii)** to make sure that the children are reading with accuracy and confidence before allowing them to attempt it in parts;
>
> **(iv)** to ensure that success is guaranteed.

Skill/Concept

3   Introducing 'MUSIC IN OUR LIVES'

▷ The introductory section 'The place of music in everyday life' can be found on page 11 of this Teacher's Book. It is well worth considering with the children the everyday circumstances in which one will find music (i) central to a situation (e.g. a concert; hymn practice); (ii) an integral part (e.g. a film); or (iii) as an adjunct (e.g. music in a supermarket). Discussion could range to other aspects of music in our lives. For instance:

- Are the children affected by music? In what ways?
- What kind of people earn their living from music? Who are the music makers?
- Why does the dentist's surgery play recorded music?
- Why do people sing in the bath?

Music activities

KEY ▶

3 a   If possible, listen to recorded and live examples of 'mood music' – music that deliberately sets out to define a particular mood or atmosphere. Ask the children to write about an example, trying to identify the essential musical qualities/elements that created the mood.
Suggestions for listening: a movement from 'La Mer' ('The Sea') by Debussy, or one of the 'Four C Interludes' by Britten.

3 b   Ask the children to use known melodies and experiment with their performance. Can a melody be made to feel sad or sombre, happy or optimistic? Can it be used for dance or for a relaxed evening by candlelight? What are the features of melody and its performance which contribute to mood and atmosphere?

☆ Pupil's Book 3, page 5

3 c   The task on page 5 of Pupil's Book 3 seeks to heighten children's awareness of the ways in which a mood is created by an appropriate choice of tempo, dynamics, timbre and expressive nuances.

Skill/Concept

4 | The whole note

▷ We now consider, aurally and visually, the whole note rhythm element
(𝅝) and its rest (▬). Traditional hymn melodies demonstrate extremely
well the use of sustained notes, such as the whole note. Voices and the
organ easily sustain notes of long duration, and without loss of volume;
however, some instruments, such as the piano, cannot do this effectively.

Suggested songs

30   Rise, sun, awaken

Music activities

KEY ▶

4 | a   Teach the children the song 'Rise, sun, awaken'. Ask the children to
identify the words which have notes of a 4-beat length (they will be
helped by tapping the pulse or beating time). The children should now
tap the rhythms of these phrases and speak 'ta-a-a-a' for the whole notes.

4 | b   Improvise phrases (such as **U5–U7**) which include half notes and whole
notes, which the children (or an individual) repeat by speaking rhythm
names:

   (i) a sung monotone;

   (ii) an instrument whose sound can be sustained and dampened
   (e.g. an electronic keyboard, or metallophone);

or **(iii)** melodic improvising with instrument or voice.

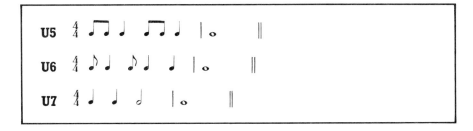

Ask individual children to improvise in a similar way.

Play the game 'Spot the composer' to incorporate whole notes. Several
children in turn improvise a rhythm-phrase which is immediately written
in notation on the board. The name of the composer is put at the side of
each one. Subsequently, a child elects to perform one of these rhythms.
The class decide which melody has been used.

4 | c   Play to the children traditional hymn tunes which feature whole notes
played on an organ (or other suitable instrument). Can they identify the
whole notes? Explain to the children that a hymn is usually a religious
song, and an important feature of most forms of Christian worship.

☆ Pupil's Book 3,
   page 6

EXTENSION ▶

4 d **U8–U11** will provide reading practice from the board, or could be used for dictation purposes. Encourage individual children to improvise a suitable extension to the given phrase(s), and then to write down their extended melody.

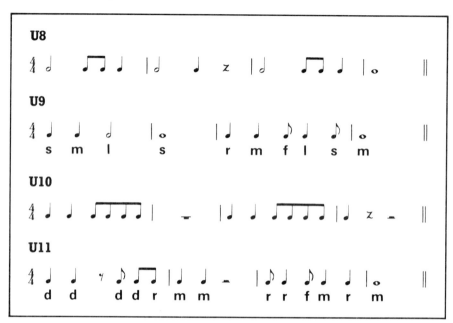

4 e After singing 'Rise, sun, awaken', ask the children to read and tap a 4-beat rhythm-phrase selected from rhythm cards or from a series of phrases on the board at those points in the song where whole notes occur.

4 f Investigate the religious music of non-Christian religions, e.g. the Hindu Bhajan and the Islamic Qawali. Local advisers for music and multi-cultural education will be able to suggest appropriate materials and assistance from local sources.

Skill/Concept

5 Composing with the whole note

▷ Page 7 of Pupil's Book 3 is concerned with using the whole note in composing. It is at this stage that 'appropriateness', 'balance' and 'style' will become increasingly important as the children construct melodies of growing complexity.

Suggested songs

12 Grandfather still you may see at a party
14 Infant holy
16 I've a grey horse
24 Oh the praties they grow small
27 Planting rice
31 Speed bonnie boat

> ▷ **Constructing melody:** The architecture of a melody can help significantly to create a sympathetic response in the mind of the performer or listener; for example, when the melody has an attractive line and shape, and when there is a sense of balance and appropriateness between the various phrases. Melody has always had a strong need for 'going in the right direction', having a good 'line'; having high moments (climax) and relaxed moments (repose); gathering momentum through repeated short phrases performed successively higher or lower (sequence) to attain points of climax or repose. The refrain of the song 'I've a grey horse' exemplifies these ideas concisely. The song 'Planting rice' has very good examples of sequence in 4-bar phrases; 'Oh the praties they grow small' has a balanced phrase structure (A B A) and points of appropriate climax and response in phrases B, A. Further examples can be found in 'Infant holy', 'Grandfather still you may see at a party', 'Speed bonnie boat' and many others.

Music activities

KEY ▶

5 **a** It is suggested that known songs (see the above list for examples) should be sung to help illustrate and explore the ideas of line, shape, sequence, climax, repose and balance. Ask the children to trace the shape of successive and individual phrases with their hands. Draw the shape of selected phrases with a continuous line on the board in order to consider their shape and to make comparisons between phrases.

5 b Sing the hymn 'Morning has broken' with the children (not in this Song collection). Discuss the phrase structure and the melodic content and encourage them to recognise the important part played by the shape of the melodic line and the balance of phrases in making the hymn musically successful. In particular, examine the first two phrases – how each moves to a point of higher pitch to achieve a sense of climax and then proceeds to finish on a point of lower pitch (repose). Reinforce this by drawing with fingers in the air, or by appropriate line shapes on the board.

☆ Pupil's Book 3,
page 7

5 c It can be a pleasurable and recurring occasion to teach to the whole school songs which have been composed by the children. At the end of the year some form of acknowledgement might be made for the song(s) most enjoyed.

Perhaps some of the composed hymns could be sung in the school assembly.

Skill/Concept

6 Working with canons

▷ The musical device known as **canon** has always been regarded as a challenging part of a composer's craft and an immensely pleasurable experience for performers. Canons have been sung and played for many centuries, one of the earliest examples being the famous 13th-century canon 'Summer is icumen in'.

The word canon literally means 'rule'. The rule here is that the voice which begins the melody shall be closely imitated, note for note by a second voice – see the first of the examples on page 8 in the Pupil's Book. However, in the second example on page 8 of Pupil's Book 3 the second voice imitates the first, not at the unison, but a note higher – an interval of a second – and is therefore said to be a canon at the second.

Music activities

KEY ▶

6 a Singing a known example of a song with a pentatonic tone-set, ask a first group of children to begin, followed by a second group starting several beats later and singing the same melody. Experiment with the entry point of the second voice to find the most satisfying version. Songs such as 'One for the mouse' and 'Engine, engine, number nine' (Key Stage 2A, song 36) are useful examples.

6 b Sing the pentachordal song, 'Once a man fell in a well' (see Key Stage 1, song 35 and Key Stage 2A, song 54) with the second group starting two beats later. Then try with a second entry only one beat later than the first group.

6 c Response canons. These ask a second voice group/individual to respond aurally and sing a canon begun by a first voice. The first voice reads or improvises, but the second voice always performs from listening only. **U12–U14** provide written examples for the first voice to use.

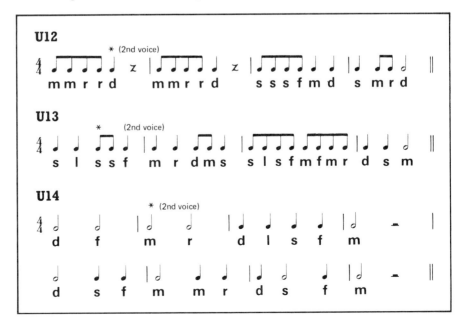

6 d To prepare the children for reading, singing and understanding canons that ask the second voice to imitate at a different pitch, sing a short phrase and ask the children to echo at a pitch which is one note higher. **U15–U16** provide several examples.

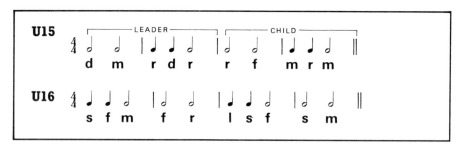

Ask a child to echo a given phrase one note higher or lower, beginning on the last note of the phrase, as in Examples **U17–U18**.

Encourage confidence in this skill by first repeating the phrase as a sequence, one note higher or lower as appropriate. Then establish the point of entry for the child and confirm the first note of the response part.

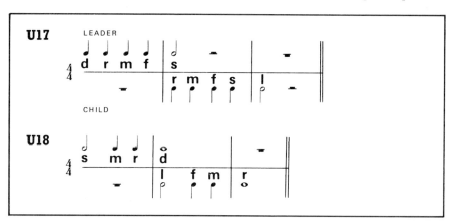

☆ **Pupil's Book 3, pages 8 and 9**

6 e Page 9 provides a more developed and extended example of canon. Since the rhythm element ♩. has not yet been introduced (see Pupil's Book 3, page 24) it will be necessary to explain that these notes must be sustained for three beats.

6 f Starting a choral music file. We are now ready for the first items from the children's Choral files (see Copymasters pages 197–215). These are for the children to read and sing. The children should keep their copies in their own Music files, as a resource which can be used for review purposes and performances.

6 g ☆ Choral file 1: 'All night long'

Be sure the children sing notes to their full rhythmic value, especially during the first four bars. Alternating parts (as in bars 1–4) can lead to ragged entries. If this happens, ask all the children to sing both parts to create the idea of a continuous phrase, rhythmically accurate and within a strict tempo.

6 h ☆ Choral file 2: 'Warm days'

Ask the children to sing the melody only (lower part, bars 1–4; upper part, bars 5–8) so they are aurally aware of the complete melody and of its position when singing in parts. Carefully tune the opening notes of both parts, to ensure accurate intonation.

Skill/Concept

7 **A new note – low lah (l,). Da Capo al Fine**

▷ Here the children are introduced to a new note – low lah (l,). The handsign is the same as for 'lah', but placed in a position below 'doh'.

Suggested songs

 9   Give me oil in my lamp
26   Past three o'clock
31   Speed bonnie boat

Music activities

KEY ▶

7 a   Teach 'Give me oil in my lamp'. Ask the children to sing the first phrase only to solfa and to identity the 'new note' by humming and sustaining it. Name the note 'low lah' and explain to the children that it is sung as 'lah' with a supporting handsign using the known 'lah' shape, but appearing in a position below doh. The children now repeat the phrase to solfa with supporting handsigns.

7 b   Improvising with l, can be done by selecting previous teaching ideas. Here are some more:

- The teacher hums a phrase using known pitch names, including low lah. The children repeat, but singing to solfa.
- The teacher writes on the board a rhythm with a pitch reference as shown, and the children perform accordingly. The children could experiment by devising new pitch references.

Pitch reference: $\quad \downarrow = l, \quad \square = d \quad \downarrow = m \quad \downarrow\downarrow\ \downarrow = r$

- Ask four children to improvise a melody with an A A B A structure. Each phrase – A and B – should feature the new note.

7 c   Sing the songs 'Captain, go side-track your train' and 'There was an old woman' (see Key Stage 2A, songs 44 and 45). Both these songs feature l,. Can the children identify where the new note is used?

☆ Pupil's Book 3,
   page 10

7 d

A new feature introduced by page 10 is the use of the term '*Da Capo al Fine*'. This is a labour saving (and paper saving!) device for music written with an A B A or A A B A structure. The 'Goblin song' is a good example. The Italian words mean 'from the beginning to the finish'. There are many other songs which have this kind of structure and therefore can be written out using '*Da Capo al Fine*'; for example 'Oh dear! What can the matter be?', 'Give me oil in my lamp', 'Speed bonnie boat' and 'Past three o'clock'. Perform Reading Sheet 1A (Copymaster page 174) which also features the '*Da Capo al Fine*'.

The 'Goblin song' melody begins with an **anacrusis** – an eighth note before the first bar line. The anacrusis is the next item in the Skill/Concept index.

Skill/Concept

8 The anacrusis (or 'pick-up' note)

▷ The 'Goblin song' in the Pupil's Book introduces another new feature. Some melodies begin with a note before the first strong beat, known as an anacrusis (or 'pick-up' note). In songs, this rhythm results from the natural word stress of the sentence or phrase in the text. In written music the note value of the anacrusis is traditionally subtracted from the total note value of the last bar of the piece (see the melodies in Pupil's Book 3, page 11).

Suggested songs

11 Good morning, Missa Potter
18 Me father kept a boarding house
22 Oh me dad was a fisherman bold
KS2A 118 I saw three ships

Music activities

KEY ▶

8 a If the children tap their knees for the first beat in a $\frac{4}{4}$ metre, their shoulders for the other beats and sing such songs as 'God rest you merry gentlemen', 'Oh me dad was a fisherman bold' or 'I walked to the top of the hill' (see Key Stage 2A, song 113), they would sing the first note on the fourth beat quite naturally. Hence the rhythm:

God   rest you mer - ry,   gen - tle - men

However, in a $\frac{2}{4}$ metre the first note is often an eighth note before the stress. So in 'Good morning, Missa Potter' the rhythm is felt as $\frac{2}{4}$ ♪ | ♫ ♫ | ♫ . With appropriate tapping, ask the children to feel the anacrusis as they sing these or similar songs, e.g. 'Should auld acquaintance be forgot'.

8 b The eighth note anacrusis occurs in $\frac{6}{8}$ compound rhythm songs such as 'Me father kept a boarding house'.

- With appropriate tapping, encourage the children to feel the anacrusis as they sing this or similar songs.
- Ask the children to mark the pulse with the unpreferred hand tapping the first beat on the table and each second beat on the shoulder as the preferred hand taps the rhythm of a compound rhythm song with phrases starting with an anacrusis, e.g. 'I saw three ships come sailing in' (Reading Sheet 12).

8 c Perform tapped and spoken improvised rhythm-phrases beginning with the anacrusis, which the children repeat. Work in simple and compound times with both eighth and quarter note anacruses. Then encourage individual children to lead in a similar way. Make sure a tapped pulse is gently heard and felt throughout. Improvised examples could be written down with phrase marks and bar lines shown.

☆ Pupil's Book 3, page 11

Skill/Concept

9 **Low lah (l,) in staff notation and rhythm-solfa**

▷ The children's experience in reading is extended to include the new note l,.

Music activities

KEY ▶

9 a ☆ Reading Sheets 1B and 2

Care should be taken to prepare the children by establishing the pitch range and tempo, noticing where l, occurs and singing through each part separately to solfa in order to secure the children's confidence before attempting the two parts simultaneously. Each part should be performed several times with benefit to confidence and to aural awareness of the new note. Invite pairs of children to perform. It is possible that the children will recognise the song melodies in Reading Sheets 1B, 2A and 2B from earlier work in Key Stage 2A. When words are sung, the part without words can use solfa – or an arrangement of words derived from the song.

☆ Pupil's Book 3, page 12

9 b In working with the second example on page 12 (written by Z Kodály) the children will need to be aware of l, in relation to doh on a keyboard instrument. Using (in turn) doh = F, G and C, ask a child to sing melodic phrases based on **m–r–d–l,** and then to play each one on a keyboard without delay, while the memory is clear. Low lah is D when doh = F, E when doh = G, A when doh = C.

☆ Pupil's Book 3, page 13

9 c Invite a child to improvise a phrase vocally, using the notes **m–r–d–l,,** which a second child then plays on a keyboard instrument.

9 d Ask a child to play a phrase on a keyboard instrument using **m–r–d–l,** which the class repeat, singing to solfa.

EXTENSION ▶

9 e ☆ Writing Sheet 2

Using ♩ ♩ ♩ rhythm values and **m–r–d–l,** hum improvised phrases of 2 and 4 bars, such as **U19–U20**. The children repeat and memorise the example before writing in rhythm-solfa on Writing Sheet 2.

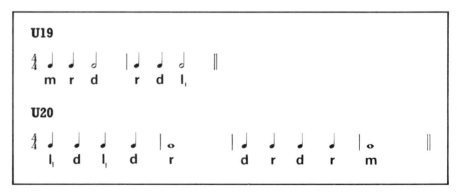

9 | f ☆ Choral file 3: 'Who's that?'

> With Choral file items, consideration should be given to the nature of
> each piece so that the most appropriate tempo, phrasing, dynamics
> and vocal style is achieved. In this process, the children's own
> thoughts should be encouraged. Pieces should be attempted in a
> variety of ways so that useful and objective debate is generated.
> Finally, suitable musical terms and marks of expression and tempo
> could be pencilled in the children's copies to aid memory.

Skill/Concept

10   For a story: the giant and the slaves

▷ Music can help to illustrate a story, as for example in a song, musical, opera or ballet. Music alone cannot tell a story, only suggest one, although some composers have depicted a sequence of episodes from a story using music, most notably Richard Strauss in 'Don Quixote'.

Music can augment the mood that the words are concerned with, and indeed strengthen the key words and phrases in a story. That is why we have so many successful and moving songs in every style.

Music activities

KEY ▶

10 a   From their song repertoire, ask the children to suggest songs in which the music is appropriate for the mood of the words and significantly illustrates the meaning of particular words. Consider with the children how much the success of an example depends on the structure of the music and the way the song is performed.

10 b   Write a sentence on the board in which the words evoke a distinctive atmosphere and situation.

Examples:
The laughter of spring is heard in the bubbling brook.
Long dark limbs of the leafless tree embrace the cold of the winter's day.

Ask individual children to improvise a vocal melody for the words. The child may wish to select a tone-set to work with. Make sure the child first 'tunes up' by singing the notes of the chosen tone-set. (On other occasions, encourage individuals to start improvising without a preconceived tone-set.)

Discuss the improvisation with the improviser and the class. What were the more positive elements of the improvisation?

☆ Pupil's Book, page 14

For improvising of this kind the children can find the words from books or even devise their own sentences.

10 c   Listen to and discuss with the children the following dramatic and powerful pieces of music:
  i) 'Erlkönig' ('Earl King'), a song by Franz Schubert, who set Goethes' words to music;
  ii) 'In the hall of the Mountain King', Grieg's incidental music to Ibsen's play *Peer Gynt*.

Skill/Concept

11 Tied notes

▷ The effect of creating an awareness of 'tied' notes will be to open up many more rhythm possibilities into the children's music activity, leading to an understanding of syncopation and paving the way to introducing dotted rhythm elements, such as $\downarrow.\flat$ and $\sqrt{}$.

Suggested songs

4 Cadet Rouselle
9 Give me oil in my lamp
20 My old hammer
27 Planting rice is never fun

Music activities

KEY ▶

11 a Teach the song 'My old hammer' in the following way:

   (i) The children walk a circle with the teacher in the centre. With the children marking a steady pulse as they walk, the teacher sings phrases to 'nah' for the children to repeat.

   (ii) Perform again in a similar way, but this time the children add a clap to each first pulse in a $\frac{4}{4}$ metre, supported if necessary by the teacher playing a tambour. Do not forget that the song starts with an incomplete bar.

   (iii) Sing the complete song with words as the children walk, clap and listen.

   (iv) Play the melody on an instrument capable of sustained sounds, as the children walk, clap and listen.

   In discussion ask the children if they are aware of the sustained sounds crossing over into the first and second beats of a new group of 4 beats.

☆ Pupil's Book 3, page 15

11 b The Pupil's Book example begins with an anacrusis using two eighth notes.

   Other song melodies which begin in a similar way are 'Have you ever, ever, ever?' (see Key Stage 2A, song 25), 'Give me oil in my lamp' and 'Planting rice' in simple time. In compound time, 'Cadet Rousselle' begins with a $\sqrt{}$ anacrusis.

11 c **U21–U23** will provide visual reinforcement for tied notes. (**U21b** is the rhythm of 'My old hammer'.)

U21–U23 should first be presented, read and spoken with rhythm names in version **a**. Then the ties are added and the new rhythm spoken as shown in version **b**. The children should tap a steady pulse as they perform the examples.

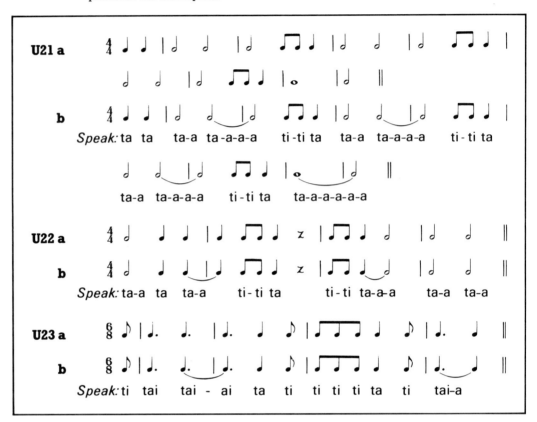

EXTENSION ▶

11 d For further examples individual children could improvise other rhythm pieces which are written on the board. A version with tied notes might then be suggested, preferably through improvising, and the ties written in.

11 e ☆ **Reading Sheet 3A**

This reading sheet gives further practice in performing with low lah and tied notes.

Skill/Concept

12 Melodies based on l,

▷ After the children have worked with doh-based melodies which move down to low lah, they can be helped to distinguish between doh-based melodies and melodies which are actually based on l, (of minor tonality). Through performance and discussion the expressive qualities of lah- and doh-based melodies can be considered and compared. In addition to those given in the Pupil's Book, other useful melodies are 'Me father kept a boarding house' (l, based) and 'Give me oil in my lamp' (d based).

Suggested songs

9   Give me oil in my lamp
18 Me father kept a boarding house

Music activities

KEY ▶

12 a Ask the children to sing these melodic phrases. The first is based on l,, the second on 'doh'. They should be performed with little break between them.

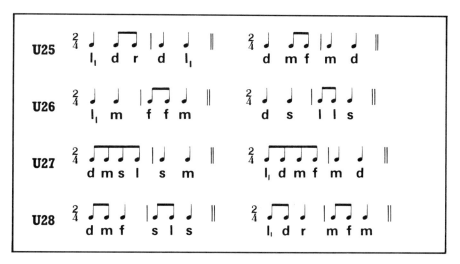

Hum a lah- or doh-based melodic phrase which the children (or a child) perform to solfa in order to identify the base note.

The children should sing and compare these lah-based and doh-based phrases:

☆ Pupil's Book 3,
  page 16

12 b Ask individual pupils to improvise short melodic phrases, based on 1, and using the tone-set **s–m–r–d–l,**. Members of the class are asked to memorise two of these, as they are sung – and then to perform them as an A B B A (or A B A B) melody.

12 c Hum **U29–U31**. The children repeat, using solfa; and then sing the lah-based (or doh-based) version. Both versions are then written in staff notation.

Skill/Concept

|13| Composing with l₁

▷ Composing is the creative musical craft at work. The act of composing often needs a stimulus; where possible, a purpose or occasion for music should provide the setting for the child's composing. Finished work should be performed and, when appropriate, kept in a child's file to record progress and to show or perform to parents.

Music activities

KEY ▶

|13| **a** Show the children that contrasting moods can be obtained from doh or lah-based melodies. The mood is often governed by the nature of words in a song, so it is sometimes useful to present a melody without its words. Perform an instrumental melody several times, changing the tempo, dynamics and pitch for successive performances to discover whether there are feelings of changed mood or not. It is possible that the children might conclude that lah-based melody has more expressive potential for reflective and sombre moods.

☆ Pupil's Book 3, page 17

|13| **b** The time signature, pitch, rhythm and structure elements given for composing on page 17 of the Pupil's Book, along with many similar ideas suggested by the children, might be written on different coloured cards (to identify the category to which they each belong) and placed in a 'composing bag'. Cards could then be selected to create a new composing task for an individual or for the class as a whole.

New cards could be added to the composing bag as new elements are encountered.

EXTENSION ▶

|13| **c** ☆ Reading Sheet 3

Skill/Concept

14 A new note – low soh (s,)

▷ Low lah having been well established, low soh is a natural extension. Since many doh-based melodies have a pitch range of s,–s the children will become aware of a significant increase of available melodies in terms of quantity and expressive quality.

Suggested songs

The following songs from the **Key Stage 2A** Song collection will have given the children useful experience in singing with both l, and s,:

48   Circle left, old red waggon
49   Hill an' gully ride-a
51   Chu, lu, lu
91   Chatter with the angels
92   No one in the house
105 What shall I do?

In addition, the following titles to be found in **Key Stage 2B** Song collection prominently feature the l, and s, notes:

24   Oh, the praties they grow small
31   Speed bonnie boat

Music activities

KEY ▶

14 **a**   The song 'Chatter with the angels' (**Key Stage 2A**, song 91) features both l, and the new note, low soh (s,). Once the children have been reminded of the song, they should attempt the first phrase to solfa at a slower tempo, discovering the new note, linking it with the soh handsign in a position below l, and then continuing with the succeeding phrases.

In addition, sing the popular song 'Old Macdonald had a farm' to solfa, starting on 'doh' and at a slow tempo in order to discover the prominent use of low soh and the tone-set **m–r–d–l,–s,**.

14 **b**   Reading. **U32–U36** are rhythm-solfa examples featuring low soh. These and similar examples should be read and sung by the children from the board. To add interest, ask an individual child to sing the complete example with the class, but the class using 'thinking voices' for low 'lahs' and 'sohs'. Also, repeat these phrases, with a change of pitch.

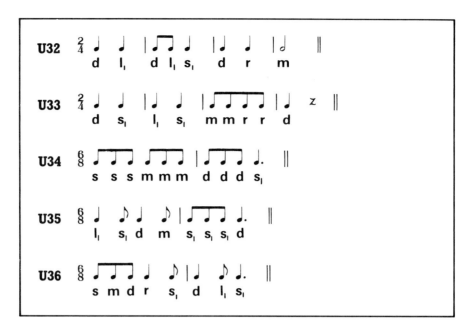

☆ Pupil's Book 3,
page 18

14 c A child improvises a phrase to solfa which includes low soh. The class repeats it at a new starting pitch determined by the teacher.

14 d Working in pairs, the first child improvises a phrase to solfa; the second child provides an answering phrase which must start on the last note of the first phrase. Both phrases must feature low lah and low soh.

14 e **U37–U40** are examples of staff notation which can be read from the board.

Never allow the reading and performing of short pieces of music and exercises to become dull and mechanical. Continually challenge the children to perform with specified tempo and dynamic indications and to contribute ideas as to how an example could be performed.

14 f ☆ Reading Sheet 4

In 4B, note the use of repeat marks. The first time bar ⌐1——————⌐ is omitted in the repeat and the second time bar ⌐2—————⌐ performed instead.

14 g Dictation. Invent suitable short phrases for dictation, featuring l, and s,. The children should always repeat the phrase, using solfa before writing in staff notation.

14 h ☆ Choral file 4: 'Old House'

Skill/Concept

15 Upper and lower parts of the pentatone

▷ Pages 19, 20 and 21 in Pupil's Book 3 are concerned with wider pitch-range melodies in which the individual phrases are often constructed within either the upper or the lower sections of the pentatone.

Music activities

KEY ▶

15 **a** Sing the melody of 'Rap-a-tap-a' from Reading Sheet 2A. The first two phrases are in the upper section of the pentatone, the third and fourth phrases are in the lower section.

(i) Sing through the song.

(ii) Identify the notes used in each phrase by singing to solfa. Write on the board the tone-set for the song.

(iii) Work with handsigns to remind the children about the structure and sound of the pentatone, and explore its vocal range to include l, (l–s–m–r–d–l,).

(iv) Show how each phrase falls into one of the two sections of the tone-set:

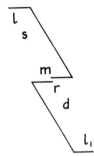

☆ **Pupil's Book 3,**
   pages 19 and 20

The three notes in each section have the same pitch relationship. For example:

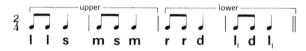

15 b In the song 'Hill an' gully ride-a' (Key Stage 2A, song 49) the section of the tone-set used for each phrase can be clearly seen and heard.

  (i) Sing through the song.

  (ii) Identify the notes used in each phrase by singing to solfa. Write on the board to build up the tone-set for the song.

  (iii) Work with handsigns to remind the children about the structure and sound of the pentatone, and explore its vocal range to include l, and s, (l–s–m–r–d–l,–s,).

  (iv) Show how each phrase falls into one of the two sections of the tone-set:

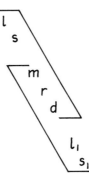

☆ Pupil's Book 3,
page 21

Other songs can be explored in a similar way, e.g. 'Me father kept a boarding house' and, if available, 'Land of the silver birch'.

15 c ☆ Reading Sheet 4C

The children should learn both parts and be able to sing them from memory. Then, as a classroom orchestra, one group plays the upper part on instruments of similar timbre and another group plays the lower part on instruments of a different timbre. G doh or F doh will be the most appropriate. Use instruments which can sustain the half note.

15 d ☆ Reading Sheet 5

The first is an interesting example of Bantu melody, sung in canon, which moves between the lower and upper sections of the tone-set. Example 5B uses the melody of 'Westminster chimes'. Both parts can be performed simultaneously by one child.

15 e ☆ Choral files 4 and 5

These pieces have very different moods and will require contrasting styles of performance. Tempo, dynamics and expression will have to be considered carefully, as well as the style of singing. 'Old house' benefits from firm attack and detached notes. The children will need to make their consonants short and crisp. 'Sleep, baby, sleep' requires a gentle sound, with wide open vowels and a legato style.

Skill/Concept

16 Repetition and sequence

▷ *Repetition* is a simple concept, but children need to be aware of its considerable effectiveness as a device. In fact, repetition is essential to the concepts of structure and form. The concepts of same and different were first explored in Teacher's Book 2A, with regard to phrase in particular.

Sequence is repetition with a pitch difference. The concept was first encountered on page 26 (where the pitch change was by step) and on page 28 (canon). However, the pitch change can be by larger interval. It is best to work aurally with the children so that they discover for themselves what is possible.

Suggested songs

12   Grandfather still you may see at a party
14   Infant holy
16   I've a grey horse
27   Planting rice is never fun
31   Speed bonnie boat

Music activities

KEY ▶

16 a   Show by aural and written examples what is meant by sequence. For example:

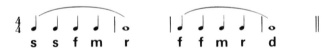

Working aurally and using **U41** ask a child to repeat the motif in sequence, keeping within the designated tone-set. Sing to solfa. The class repeats the motif and subsequent sequence. **U42–U44** are further examples.

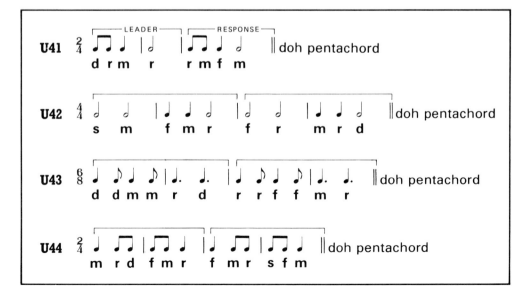

☆ **Pupil's Book 3, page 22**

16 b   Many songs in the Song collections of Key Stage 2 will provide aural and written illustrations of sequence. For example, from Key Stage 2B see those songs listed under 'Suggested songs' above. Look out for other melodies such as the Welsh traditional melody 'The Ash Grove'.

16 c   Working within the doh hexachord a child invites a friend to follow his/her improvised sung motif, e.g. $\frac{2}{4}$ ♫ ♫ | ♩ z ‖ , by singing and

> m r m s   f

repeating the motif in sequence either higher or lower, as indicated, e.g.

$\frac{2}{4}$ ♫ ♫ | ♩ z ‖   lower. The children should work with phrases

> r d r f   m

☆ **Pupil's Book 3, page 23**

of 4-beat length in both simple and compound time.

Skill/Concept

17 ¾ time

▷ The simple time metres of 2 (2/4) and the compound time metre of 2 (6/8) are already familiar to the children. Remind them that it is from the performing of rhythm that a regular pulse is felt, and it is from rhythm that the comparative strengths of the pulse are sensed and give rise to a pattern of strong and weak pulses known as the metre. We now introduce the simple time metre of 3 (¾).

In notation, metre is shown by writing 2/4 or 3/4 or 4/4 or 6/8 at the beginning of the piece. This is called the **time signature**.

Suggested songs

Some of the songs from the **Key Stage 2B** Song collection having a metre of 3 beats are:

 3 Brian Ó Linn
 5 Cagaran, cagaran
14 Infant holy
26 Past three o'clock

Music activities

KEY ▶

☆ **Pupil's Book 3,**
    page 24

17 **a** Sing known songs which have a metre of 3 beats; identify the pattern of 3 beats by tapping appropriately the strong and weak pulses and make a written list of the titles of such songs (see list above).

The children should sing and conduct with a hand moving thus:

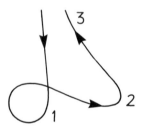

17 **b** A succession of melodies with differing metres is sung or played by the teacher or a child. Each individual in the class is asked to accompany the melodies by tapping on a table with the palm upwards for the steady pulse and by a tap with the palm downwards for the strong beat.

17 **c** Listen to recordings or a live performance of music which feature the simple time metre of 3. For example:
    ● a 17th or 18th century minuet (Purcell, Handel, Haydn etc.);
    ● a 19th century waltz, e.g. 'The Blue Danube';
    ● a popular 20th century song, e.g. 'Moon River' or 'Oom-pah-pah!' (from *Oliver!*).

17 **c**   Working in groups, the children list known melodies under the headings:

Simple time		Compound time	
Song title	Metre (2, 3 or 4)	Song title	Metre (2 only)

One group then challenges another group to identify the metre of a melody from their list, performed by the group or a member of the group.

17 **d**   Reading and writing. **U45**–**U49** give examples using the 3/4 time signature which could be written on the board, read and performed. Rhythms containing ♩ / ♩. are better dictated or read using either rhythm-names or by singing on a monotone. The 3-beat note ♩. is spoken as 'ta-a-a'.

Any of the examples could be used for writing from dictation; **U47**–**U49** should be sung on a monotone to 'doo', giving slight emphasis to the first beat note of each bar.

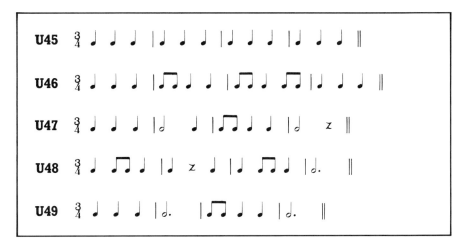

EXTENSION ▶

17 **e**   Improvising: ask a first child to improvise a rhythm phrase with a simple time metre of 3. A second child then repeats the rhythm but, by singing or playing an instrument, adds a pitch element to create an improvised melody.

17 **f**   ☆ Reading Sheets 6, 7 and 8

(i) Reading Sheets 6 and 7 provide longer melodies. Notice the anacrusis in examples (7B) and (7C), and the various use of repeat marks, *Da Capo al Fine*, and first time/second time bars in (7A) and (7B). Examine examples 6A, 6C and 7B for incidences of sequence, and examples 6B, 6D and 7A for phrase structure.

It is well worth performing the rhythm only to rhythm-names at first.

(ii) Reading Sheet 8A is a two-part arrangement of an American folk melody. The melody is l, based and begins with an anacrusis.

(iii) Reading Sheet 8B features l, and s,.

Skill/Concept

18 **For a story: the cheerful old woman**

▷ Everyone can recall a catalogue of domestic disasters such as those experienced by the old woman in the song on Pupil's Book 3, page 25. The old woman's reactions to such incidents may not be typical of our own! We can presume that her life carried on more normally in between. In this respect the song begins to suggest the structure of a theatre piece such as a musical, in which the same music reappears at several points in the play (reprises), but with new words reflecting new circumstances.

Music activities

KEY ▶
☆ Pupil's Book 3,
  page 25

18 **a** To use instruments as proposed on the Pupil's Book page, it will be necessary to teach some instrumentalists, by rote, to play this accompaniment.

EXTENSION ▶ **18** **b** ☆ Worksheet 1 (page 165)

48

Skill/Concept

19 Fixed pitch – the doh pentachord

▷ Ask the children to work on their own with the activities on Pupil's
Book 3, page 26, without any preparation as a class group.

Music activities

KEY ▶
☆ Pupil's Book 3, page 26

19 **a** Check that the children understand the fixed pitch names by working with
individuals and the class as a whole.

19 **b** Establish with the children whether C doh pentachord or G doh
pentachord is being used and then hum an improvised motif or short
phrase. The children (or child) repeat(s), first singing to solfa, then to fixed
pitch names – and finally play(s) the phrase on an instrument.

EXTENSION ▶

19 **c** Using an electronic keyboard, ask the children to discover what happens
when doh pentachords start on notes other than C and G (i.e. it becomes
necessary to use some black notes).

Skill/Concept

20 | The treble clef

▷ Up to this stage, the children have become very aware that doh may be sung at any pitch – and that, as a symbol in staff notation, doh may be placed at any point on the staff. It is important that the children continue to use solfa and the movable doh as common vocal practice. However, fixed pitch concepts are now being taught, and in working vocally with fixed pitch the teacher should take care at all times to pitch correctly. In other words, the note G in staff notation should always be the note G when sung. (Obviously, this is automatic when using instruments.)

The clef (treble, bass, etc.) in staff notation fixes the pitch of the notes. The function of the G clef (or treble clef) is only to show where the note G is situated on the staff – it does not show the position of doh, or give any other solfa reference. So, from this stage onwards, the solfa name of the first note of each melody is always given as a reference for vocal reading. Reading with an instrument directly relates to the fixed pitch name.

Music activities

KEY ▶

20 a Individual attention will be needed with some children to reinforce the connection between the notes on the staff and notes on the instrument. Also, some children will need help in understanding that the letters A–G are used in a repeated, circular form. The use of the flying note on a staff showing the G clef may be helpful here. Teachers can find an explanation of the flying note idea in the Key Stage 2A Course programme. Having established a tone-set of 3 or 4 notes, point to the relevant part of the staff with the flying note. The children sing the fixed pitch names as the flying note is used. Finally, they play the melodic phrase on an instrument.

☆ Pupil's Book 3, page 27

20 b The children should be given time to explore with their instruments the range of 9 notes which the joined pentachords provide. They will need practice in relating letter names to particular keys on the keyboard. For example, the children could be encouraged to play a series of notes and sing the relevant letter names as they do so.

Skill/Concept

21 Reading with the G clef

▷ The intention of page 28 of Pupil's Book 3 is to show how staff notation can be used for vocal reading as well as instrument reading. It should encourage the habit of using the 'thinking voice' when reading with an instrument. (In other words, musical thinking guides the hands playing the instrument and guesswork has no part in the process; any mistakes accidentally played on the instrument are detected immediately by the child's listening, thinking and memory.)

Music activities

KEY ▶
☆ **Pupil's Book 3, page 28**

21 **a** The melody on page 28 moves mostly by 'step' from note to note, a helpful feature at this stage of identifying fixed pitch names.

21 **b** ☆ **Reading Sheet 9A–9C and 10A**

These provide further examples needed to encourage the 'thinking voice' process described in the introduction above. Work with the three methods of performance suggested on page 28 of Pupil's Book 3. These 'doh' pentachord melodies will also help the children become familiar with the G clef and fixed pitch names, using instruments and voices.

21 **c** As an aid to familiarising themselves with the letter names of the G clef staff, the children could use the five finger staff (see Key Stage 2A Teacher's Book page 65). Ask them to draw with a pencil a G clef in the correct place on the palm of the left hand and to finger-point the notes as they sing the letter names.

Skill/Concept

22 **The doh hexachord on C and G**

▷ The concept of the 'doh' hexachord is familiar to the children. In working with 'doh' hexachords on C and G the children will quickly realise that they are simply extensions of the 'doh' pentachords on C and G.

Music activities

KEY ▶

22 **a** Aural. The following ideas will be helpful to children in understanding the difference between the pentachord and hexachord when working with solfa or fixed pitch names:

    (i) Ask them to sing the notes of the 'doh' pentachord starting on fixed pitch C, thus: **d–r–d–m–d–f–d–s–d–f–d–m–d–r–d** – and then the notes of the hexachord in a similar way.

    (ii) Ask the children to sing the letter names of the 'doh' pentachord on C, as they point to the relevant keys or bars on their instruments, thus: **C–D–C–E–C–F–C–G–C–F–C–E–C–D–C** – and then the notes of the hexachord in a similar way.

    (iii) Work the above ideas using the 'doh' pentachord and hexachord on G.

☆ Pupil's Book 3,
page 29

22 **b** Improvising: invite the children to improvise with the voice, using fixed pitch names as well as solfa. Here are several ideas which may add interest:

● 'Marathon relay' – a child improvises a sung phrase which must start with the note 'doh' (C or G). This is followed by a different singer who starts on the next note of the hexachord (r). A third singer starts on 'me' and the game continues until six phrases have been improvised.

● 'Baton changing' – a child sings an improvised phrase which the class repeats. When the child sings to solfa the class must repeat to fixed pitch names, but to solfa if the child uses fixed pitch. It is obviously important to predetermine whether the doh hexachord is on C or G and to work within that agreed range of notes at the correct pitch.

● 'Tag duet' – working with a partner, a child improvises a sung phrase within the doh hexachord. Before the start of the first phrase the improviser names one or two notes (solfa or fixed pitch names) which the partner must include in his/her response phrase.

With any of these games, the opportunity might be taken to write down in staff notation (with treble clef) what has been improvised, with an awareness of whether the doh hexachord is on C or G.

> When improvising, encourage the children to perform with various simple time metres and compound time, and ask them to say which they will use before starting.

EXTENSION ▶

22 **c**   ☆ Reading Sheets 10B, 10C and 11

These are interesting examples for performing and analysing. Many of the concepts featured in this book appear in these examples, e.g. anacrusis, sequence, syncopation, phrase structure, canon, *Da Capo al Fine*.

22 **d**   ☆ Reading Sheet 12

This is a score for class performance using voices and instruments. Words are given with the melody line, and Parts A and B are played by instruments. The children could read from the score, or could write out the parts in staff notation. Rehearsal will be needed to ensure that the rhythmic movement of each part is precisely in phase with the rest of the ensemble.

As alternatives, two parts could be sung and one part played (in various combinations) – or all three parts could be sung, using solfa for parts A and B.

22 **e**   ☆ Choral file 6: 'Fire down below'

This piece obviously requires a bright, vivacious sound, but beware that the tone does not degenerate into a raucous shout, especially when the music is performed at the printed pitch. It might be easier for the children to produce the desired effect by singing with an F doh when performing without copies. Rhythmic vitality would be enhanced by using short, crisp consonants for the words 'Fire' and 'Fetch'.

Skill/Concept

| 23 | Folk dance and the sixteenth note |

▷ The children are here made aware of the sixteenth note (semiquavers) through aural, reading and performing activities, and of its use in vocal music and folk dance. The examples at this stage are confined to the use of the sixteenth note in simple time rhythm.

Suggested songs

7   Di didl lan dan
23 Oh the country farmer went to Montreal

Music activities

KEY ▶

23 **a**   ☆ Reading Sheets 13A and 13B

Ask the children to sing the song 'This old man he played one' as an example of hexachordal melody. Ask them to sing phrases to solfa and then to fixed pitch letter names, using doh = C. Then, read and compare Reading Sheets 13A and 13B (♫♫ = ti-ki-ti-ki).

23 **b**   There are a couple of simple time songs in the Key Stage 2B Song collection which feature the sixteenth note (see list above). It is suggested that the following procedure could be used with known song material. Ask the children to:

- Sing through selected known songs featuring the sixteenth note and tap a steady pulse as they do so.
- Select phrases from the songs containing the sixteenth note and ask the children to tap the rhythm as they mark a steady pulse with a foot tap.
- Ask the children to listen to selected phrases played on an appropriate instrument, e.g. xylophone, as a steady pulse is maintained by a tambour.
- Four-beat extracts containing the sixteenth note should then be tapped and repeated speaking rhythm names.
- Suitable four-beat rhythm extracts from known songs should first be aurally identified with rhythm names before being written on the board.

☆ Pupil's Book 3,
   pages 30 and 31

23 **c**   As much improvising, reading and writing with the sixteenth note should be undertaken as the teacher thinks necessary to consolidate the children's grasp of the new rhythm element.

EXTENSION ▶   23 **d**   Teach the children to dance selected folk dances.

23 **e**   ☆ Orchestral file 1: 'The fox and the grapes'

As the children learn to work with fixed pitch, it is important that they use the instruments increasingly, particularly in ensemble. Orchestral file 1 is the first item for their orchestral file.

> **Orchestral files**
> Each score is numbered, for reference purposes; each of the associated parts has the same number as the score and a letter, according to the number of parts. Suitable extra percussion may be added as the teacher, or performers, decide. Orchestral pieces are intended for instrumental rather than vocal performing.

☆ Orchestral file 1: 'The fox and the grapes'

Skill/Concept

24 | Music for folk dancing

▷ Children, like people of any age, enjoy getting together to celebrate, e.g. a birthday. We celebrate together in various ways, but one of the more usual is dancing – discos, barn dances, ballroom dancing and so on.

The old dance forms were devised for celebrations. These dances are numerous, varied and timeless in popularity. They reflect an aspect of human behaviour that has a distinctive and special appeal to most of us at some time or another, viz, the joining together with others to organise and share a sequence of body movements which can produce feelings of kinship, wellbeing and contentment.

Advice on English country dance is locally available to teachers, often from a local adviser or a branch of the English Folk Dance and Song Society (EFDSS). Audio and literary publications are widely available through libraries, music and book retailers. Those of the EFDSS are particularly recommended. Information, advice and workshops for the regional dance forms of England, Ireland, Scotland and Wales and for those of other cultures within the community, are locally available. Please provide children with opportunities to experience the rich variation of traditional dance.

Music activities

KEY ▶

24 a Play recordings of several dance tunes for the children to think about.

Can they hear the repetitions of some sections of the melody?
Can they decide on the structural pattern (e.g. A A B B) of each melody?
Can the children identify particular rhythm features, tap them and write them down?
What other features can the children comment on?
What instruments are being played?

24 b Listen first to a dance tune, learn the dance movements and then perform. What do the children notice about the dance movements and the structure of the music? Are they aware that a particular sequence of movements coincides with a particular part of the music structure and has the same time length?

☆ Pupil's Book,
   pages 32 and 33

EXTENSION ▶

24 c Learn a dance from at least one other region of the world or the British Isles.

24 d ☆ Choral file 7: 'Summer goodbye'

The German title is 'Winter ade!' (Winter goodbye!). These new words will require a singing style which is gentle and legato (smooth), without being weak.

If the parts are to hang together rhythmically, the voices must listen carefully to each other and maintain an even tempo. There could be a tendency for the lower part to anticipate each new phrase.

Skill/Concept

25 Melodic structure

▷ The aim is to reinforce and develop the children's understanding of melodic structure. Remind them of the part played by same and different in music, especially with regard to phrase length, phrase structure, sequence, and rhythm pattern.

Music activities

KEY ▶

☆ Pupil's Book 3,
page 34

25 a   ☆ Worksheet 2: Group composing (musical consequences)

Give out copies of Worksheet 2. Working in partners, the sequence of events is as follows:

● as instructed, compose phrase A;
● pass your sheet to a neighbouring pair;
● sing the phrase you have received;
● compose phrase B as a suitable succeeding phrase;
● pass the sheet to your neighbouring pair;
● sing the two phrases you have received;
● compose phrase C as a suitable finishing phrase;
● pass your sheet to a neighbouring pair;
● sing the three phrases you have received;
● write in staff notation the complete melody with the structure A A B C B C.

The children perform the completed melodies to the class. The class could add words to the melodies generally agreed to be the best.

☆ Pupil's Book 3,
page 35

25 b   Page 35 of the Pupil's Book reinforces the children's experience in reading two-part pieces, singing with low lah and soh, and playing instrumentally. The top piece is a traditional French folksong.

EXTENSION ▶

25 c   ☆ Reading Sheet 14A

It is always a good idea to establish aurally the tone-set used and any notable rhythmic features. The following suggestion should help to bring added interest and musical challenge, while reinforcing certain features of pitch: ask the children to sing the lower part and simultaneously to sing in their heads the upper part; then to repeat, but reversing the activities.

25 d   ☆ Choral file 8: 'Lavender's blue'

Rising intervals are more difficult to negotiate with vocal ease than descending intervals. For the following exercise the children should stand with a helpful singing posture. The piece should be sung slowly and deliberately with the diaphragm muscle being used more strongly for the rising intervals. For further practice sing the exercise using a higher starting note.

The top part voices should breathe at beat 3 of bar 4.

The following is a suggestion for an extended performance:
first time: top part only (p);
first repeat: lower part only (mp);
second repeat: both parts (f).

Skill/Concept

26 Composing by oneself

▷ Composing is now a natural extension of work already done. The children are asked to compose within clearly defined parameters, while retaining some element of choice. They should be encouraged to be critical of what they produce, to make several attempts and to improve and refine what they have written, until they have a finished product with which they are satisfied and which they would be happy to have performed. It is very important to perform finished melodies and afterwards to hear the composer's thoughts and views on the piece and its performance – before discussing the melody with the rest of the class and with the teacher. A subsequent comparison of the child's composition with known, established melodies of similar structure is extremely valuable.

All the child's compositions should be kept in his/her file for future reference and pleasure. They should be valued as a record of personal progress and achievement.

Music activities

KEY ▶
☆ Pupil's Book 3, pages 36 and 37

26 a The following could act as a checklist when considering a composing task. The items under each heading are elements the children are familiar with so far. The checklist below serves as an example. You should modify the list when necessary.

Purpose (e.g.) setting of words : Christmas Carol : echo song : canon : TV advertisement : lullaby : hymn : dance

Medium voice : keyboard : recorder : other

Structure A B : A B A : A A B B : A B B A : A B A A

Phrase lengths 2-bar phrase : 3-bar phrase : 4-bar phrase

Time signature $\frac{2}{4}$ $\frac{4}{4}$ $\frac{3}{4}$ $\frac{3}{8}$ $\frac{6}{8}$

Special rhythm features

Tone-set doh pentatone : doh pentachord on C : on G : lah pentatone : doh hexachord on C : on G : low lah : low soh

Special features anacrusis : repeat : sequence : *Da Capo al Fine*

Notation rhythm-solfa : staff

26 b Composing tasks could occasionally take the form of 'lucky dip!' Containers, each labelled with a different heading (e.g. 'time signature'), could contain a number of cards, each card with an element written on it. The children can decide the rules for playing 'lucky dip!' but once several cards have been drawn, those elements form the basis for the child's composing task. Obviously, more cards will become available as further elements are assimilated by the children.

EXTENSION ▶

26 c ☆ Orchestral file 2: 'The fisher laddie'

Skill/Concept

27 Fanfares

▷ If hosepiping of 1 metre or more in length is attached to a brass instrument mouthpiece of suitable size, with a liquid-pouring funnel at the other end of the hose, then the children's understanding of how a range of notes can be obtained from a bugle and trumpet could be demonstrated.

The mouthpiece needs to fit tightly into one end of the hosepipe while the funnel is attached to the other. The funnel helps the resonance and loudness of the note produced.

First it will be necessary for the player to produce a 'buzz' from the lips only. Making a 'buzz' is rather like pulling the lips into taut elastic bands with a small aperture in the middle and then causing them to vibrate by blowing with a fairly strong air pressure. The player will need to vary the tautness to obtain different notes from the hosepipe.

The hosepipe and funnel should be held by a partner or curled for the player to hold. The player places his/her lips into the mouthpiece and produces the 'buzz'. If a player is successful in controlling the hosepipe trumpet it may be possible for him/her to play a fanfare.

Music activities

KEY ▶
☆ Pupil's Book 3,
   page 38

27 a A visit by local players of brass instruments would show the children what impressive musical results can be achieved from the simple principles described above.

EXTENSION ▶

27 b Make a visit to a local brass band rehearsal.

Skill/Concept

28   The pentachord on l, (a new note – te)

▷ Consciously working with the note 'te' will facilitate an understanding of the lah pentachord and open up new areas of development. Hence, this is an important milestone for the children.

A good deal of aural and written work is presented here, in order to provide the teacher with a choice of teaching ideas and material and to give the children a wide range of music experience.

Music activities

KEY ▶

28 a   Pentachords can be based on a note other than doh. With the support of handsigns, show how the song 'Oh! madam, I will give to you' (Pupil's Book 3, page 41) is a pentachordal melody based on lah. Practise with the children the new note 'te' and its supporting handsign, singing: **m–r–d–t,–l,**.

28 b   With supporting handsigns, practise singing pentachords as sequences: **s–f–m–r–d/f–m–r–d–t,/m–r–d–t,–l,/r–d–t,–l,–s,**.

28 c   Sing lah pentachords up and down (l,–t,–d–r–m/m–r–d–t,–l,):

   (i) with all notes the same length;

   (ii) to the following rhythms written on the board:

   – starting on l,
   – then starting on m.

28 d Perform with the children the following Response Canons. Select one example to perform repeatedly until the children know it by heart. The children should then sing it in unison, using handsigns, before performing it as a class in two groups.

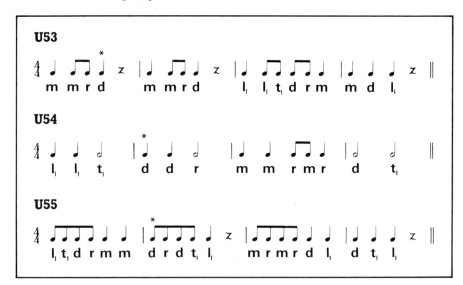

28 e These examples can be read from the board:

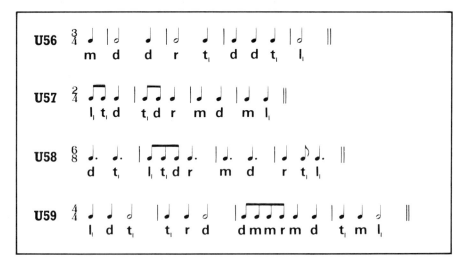

28 f Improvising: ask individual children to improvise melodic phrases using notes of the lah pentachord. To stimulate confidence employ well-tried forms of improvising. Encourage the children to use § time as well as simple time metres. As an interesting variation when improvising, the children could stand in a circle and a child holding a ball is designated the improviser. After the improvised phrase has been repeated by the class, the ball is thrown by the first child to a second who must then provide another phrase, and so on.

28 g It is useful for the children to compare aurally the doh and lah pentachords. Assign a particular note of the doh pentachord to each child in a group of 5 and ask them to sing and hold their note in the following way, so as to produce a chord cluster:

s _____
f _____
m _____
r _____
d _____

Then another group of 5 children sing the notes of the lah pentachord in a similar way. Comparisons can be made and further groups given the experience of performing.

☆ **Pupil's Book 3,
page 39**

28 h The song on page 39 celebrates the Jewish Festival of Hanukkah. There is opportunity here for performing in canon, using voices or instruments – or both together. (Page 7 of Pupil's Book 4 has another melody for Hanukkah.)

EXTENSION ▶

28 i ☆ **Reading Sheet 14**

Examples 14B and 14C are canons based on the lah pentachord. The children could read then perform, working in pairs.

Skill/Concept

29 Making a climax

▷ Music is a very powerful medium for reaching down into our innermost feelings. This is exemplified by the use that film directors make of music to heighten the emotions felt by the viewer to a film or video. Most film scenes intent on building the action to an important climax will be partnered by a similar development in the accompanying music.

Without the presence of film or drama, the ebb and flow of climax is an intrinsic feature of musical structure. Sometimes the climax is generated by the device of increased volume as in 'The Barber of Seville' overture by Rossini, or by rhythmic intensity as in 'Bolero' by Ravel, or the upward surge of the melodies so typical of Tschaikovsky's music.

Music activities

KEY ▶

29 a Ask the children to be aware of the use made of music by the makers of videos and films to create a feeling of increasing tension (climax). Can they identify the musical features in a particular instance (e.g. increasingly faster tempo)? Can they find any common factors from listening to and watching a number of episodes (e.g. rising volume level)? What kinds of episode use 'climax music' (e.g. chase scenes)?

☆ **Pupil's Book 3, page 40**

29 b The children have already worked with repetition and melodic sequence. They should be encouraged to use these devices to good effect when developing their own music with climax.

EXTENSION ▶

29 c Children might like to construct a dramatic scene to one of the compositions and perform it accompanied by the music.

Skill/Concept

30 The lah pentachord on D

▷ The oral tradition of handing down from generation to generation stories, songs, dances and games is one which is easily grasped by an adult. But it often comes as an amazing revelation to young people to realise that the story, song, dance or game they are enjoying has been popular with previous generations of children.

Social changes, especially those of the last 100 years, have meant that many customs, and the music associated with them, have gone. However, a number of old songs and dances are still with us – and new ones, often from the traditions of other countries, are always passing into our tradition as the years roll by.

Page 41 of Pupil's Book 3 represents the first conscious introduction to the tradition of folksong. The children's first introduction to the lah pentachord in staff notation is based on D. This is done for three reasons:

(i) it lies conveniently on the staff within the vocal range;

(ii) an F doh is introduced;

(iii) no sharps or flats are needed.

Music activities

KEY ▶

☆ Pupil's Book 3,
   page 41

30 **a** Improvise a short and rhythmically simple melodic phrase using the lah pentachord on D. The children repeat, singing the phrase to solfa and supported by handsigns. They sing the phrase again, but this time using absolute pitch names and the finger staff. Finally, the phrase can be played on keyboard instruments. More phrases should be similarly improvised by individual children.

30 **b** Play 'Chinese Whispers'. Sitting in several circles, ask the first child of each group to whisper a short story (maximum 30 seconds) to the next child, who then relates the story to his/her neighbour – and so on round the circle. The last person tells the story aloud to the whole group, after which the original is retold. How do the two versions compare? What does this exercise inform us about the oral tradition?

30 **c** Teach a new singing game to a small number of children only and ask them to perform the game at each outdoor playtime for a week. What happens? How many children know the game by the end of the week? Try the experiment several times. Discuss the results with the children.

30 **d** Write **U60** on the board and invite the children to perform vocally and on instruments this folksong melody from Latvia. Perform with lah = D.

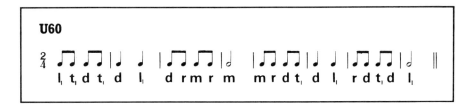

U60

l̦ ț d ț d l̦   d r m r m   m r d ț d l̦   r d ț d l̦

30 **e** Hum **U61**–**U62** for the children to write in staff notation (lah pentachord on D) – after singing to solfa, of course.

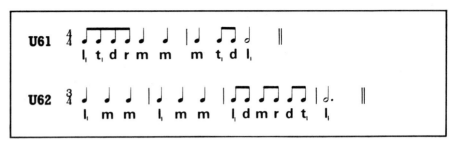

Skill/Concept

---

31 Composing with the lah pentachord

▷ Page 42 of Pupil's Book 3 encourages the children to apply their
understanding of the lah pentachord to the activity of composing. By this
stage children will have developed an aural 'feeling' for the qualities of a
lah pentachord melody, recognising them as being different from those of
a doh pentachord melody. The teaching suggestions outlined below are
intended to reinforce the feeling for the different qualities.

Music activities

KEY ▶

☆ **Pupil's Book 3,**
  page 42

31 a ☆ **Reading Sheet 15A**

Two-part examples should invariably involve performances by pairs of
individuals as well as class groups.

This is an appropriate example for two groups to perform in two parts with
each group tapping the rhythm of the other part as they sing. They then
repeat the example, exchanging the activities. This exercise encourages
the children to be aware that they are performing a two-part piece, to
listen sympathetically to another part, and to achieve rhythmic cohesion
and accurate pitching between the parts – several of the elements of good
ensemble.

Skill/Concept
---

32 **Delayed notes and passing notes**

▷ The children will have experienced aurally a great deal of music with delayed notes, and when supported by aural work along the lines suggested below, they should encounter no difficulty in reading and using such notes.

Understanding and consciously employing passing notes in the children's music making will help to create an awareness that melody is a chain of events, and very often the main structural notes on consecutive beats are connected by an intervening note or notes moving step-wise.

Avoid at this stage any theoretical explanation of passing notes and concentrate the children's minds on aural, composing and performing activities.

Suggested songs

2	As we were a-fishing
12	Grandfather still you may see at a party
13	Hot potato, pass it on
15	I was passing by
21	Now the holly bears a berry
27	Planting rice is never fun
31	Speed bonnie boat

Music activities

Delayed notes

KEY ▶

32 **a** To a tapped pulse ask the children to sing to 'nah' up and down a doh pentachord using the rhythm – ♩ ♩ ♩ ♩ ♩ ♩ etc. In imitation they now sing to the rhythm – ♩. ♪ ♩. ♪ ♩. ♪ etc. The children will notice that every other note comes after the beat. This can be visually represented on the board as ♩ ♫ ♩ ♫ ♩ ♫ etc. (see Pupil's Book 3, page 15 for tied notes) and as ♩. ♪ ♩. ♪ ♩. ♪ etc.

In a similar way the pentachord could be sung to a tapped quarter-note pulse using the rhythm – ♩ ♩ ♩ ♩ etc., followed by the delayed note version using ♩. ♩ ♩. ♩ etc. Again, this would first be represented on the board as ♩ ♩ ♩ ♩ ♩ ♩ etc. and then with dotted notes.

32 **b** Two-part scales using the notes of the doh hexachord scale and sung to 'noo' can give the children a useful and interesting experience of delayed notes. Having practised separately, both groups perform aurally to a tapped quarter-note pulse, thus:

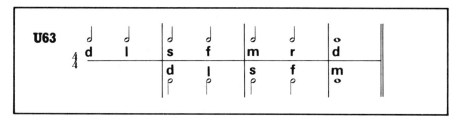

and then:

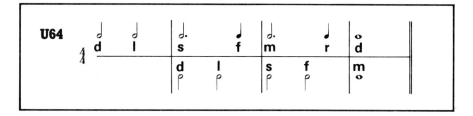

In a similar way, **U63**–**U64** could be performed using quarter-note and dotted quarter-note rhythms.

32 **c** Delayed/dotted notes will feature in many examples of the children's repertoire and it would be useful for the children to sing several prominent examples while tapping a steady pulse. Listed below are some of the songs which feature dotted notes in the Key Stage 2B Song collection.

Those featuring ♩. ♪ (simple time):

'Hot potato, pass it on'
'I was passing by'

Those featuring ♩. ♩ (simple time):

'Grandfather still you may see at a party'
'Now the holly bears the berry'

Those featuring ♩. ♪♩ (compound time):

'As we were a-fishing'
'Speed bonnie boat'

32 **d** ☆ **Reading Sheet 8A**

Read and sing Reading Sheet 8A and ask the children the following questions:

Which are the delayed notes?
How is the delay obtained in writing?
If they were not delayed, how might the music be written?

With the class write out Reading Sheet 8A, to show the delay with dotted notes.

> Explain to the children how the dot adds another half of the note length to the note it follows. Dotted and tied versions of half, quarter and eighth notes should also be shown.

Passing notes

32 e Passing notes could be introduced with the following exercise:

(i) the children read and sing with a tapped pulse at a slow tempo:

(ii) and then:

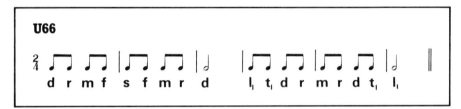

Explain that in the first version of the melody (**U65**) the notes are separated by leaps in pitch, while in the second version (**U66**) the notes 'r', 'f' and 't' link the 'leap notes' by 'filling the gaps'.

32 f Write **U67** on the board and perform it as a canon. Sing to solfa – low lah is the first note.

Show that all the notes E and G are passing notes – just filling space between two notes. Perform the canon as if there were no passing notes.

KEY ▶
☆ **Pupil's Book 3,**
page 43

32 g In working with this Pupil's Book page it is important to hear Jo's and Louise's versions of the original melody played or sung in a variety of ways (e.g. varying the tempo and dynamics; performing the notes staccato and detached or legato and smoothly), and to compare the resulting effects. Discussion with the children will hopefully conclude that the intention of the music (e.g. for a lively dance or to create a peaceful mood) will largely determine its construction and style of performance.

EXTENSION ▶

32 h It would be interesting to discover with the children prominent examples of passing notes in their repertoire. The chorus in 'Planting rice' is one such example.

Skill/Concept

33 Using delayed notes and passing notes

▷ An ability to compose with passing notes is part of the composer's craft. However, it is his/her skills in using them to effect that is important; the passing note is not a device to be worked into a melody without musical thinking and imagination.

Musical activities

KEY ▶
☆ Pupil's Book 3, page 44

33 a To help the children understand their task on page 44 of Pupil's Book 3, it might be helpful at first to work the exercise as a whole class.

33 b Invent short phrases, using the doh hexachord on C and G as well as the lah pentachord on D, for dictation – the children writing in staff notation with treble clef.

Skill/Concept

| 34 | Composing with delayed notes and passing notes |

Music activities

KEY ▶
☆ Pupil's Book 3, page 45

| 34 | a | Page 45 of Pupil's Book 3 encourages the children to make use of delayed notes and passing notes within larger melodic structures. |

| 34 | b | ☆ Orchestral file 3: 'This old man' |

Skill/Concept

35 Sporting occasion: supporters' song

▷ Supporters' chants and songs for team games have long been with us. The children will be most familiar with those associated with soccer. Many of these have melodies with origins away from the terraces. However, to some extent the words derive from the soccer fans, as do the shorter chants. A few soccer songs have at one time or another been formally composed, usually for a particular soccer team to record for publicity purposes.

Music activities

KEY ▶

35 **a** Are the children aware of supporters' songs for any sport? Can they recall them and if necessary teach them to the rest of the class? Can the children put forward reasons for these songs and why they are sung? Do the songs and chants show any common factors regarding content? What singing style is adopted for supporters' songs? Can the children name other occasions when large groups of people join together to sing? Does the singing have a similar function as the singing at sports occasions?

☆ Pupil's Book 3, page 46

35 **b** ☆ Worksheet 3

The children work with Worksheet 3 (Copymaster) which contains a complete song analysis. New analysis sheets can be found as a Copymaster in the Teacher's Book (p. 167). They are intended for use by children during Key Stage 2B as a means of recording information of an analysed piece of music or as a convenient way of setting out criteria for composing.

Skill/Concept

36 More ideas with the lah pentachord

▷ Page 47 of Pupil's Book 3 provides more opportunity for practice with the lah pentachord. It also encourages movement from the lah pentachord to the doh pentachord within the same melody. This is called **transposition** and is a useful device to children as a means of extending melodies when composing.

Music activities

KEY ▶

36 **a** Ask the children to sing to solfa the melody of the song 'Once a man fell in a well' – a doh-based melody in Key Stage 2A Song collection (no. 54); then to sing the same melody again to notes of the related lah pentachord.

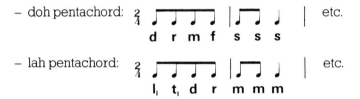

In both cases the singing should be supported by handsigns.

36 **b** The following melody can be used for the children to convert from the lah pentachord to the doh pentachord. The example should first be read and sung several times in the original with the object of memorising. After singing the melody in its doh pentachord version (starting on doh), the children should write down the melody in both versions.

☆ Pupil's Book 3,
page 47

36 **c** Ask the children to select a known pentachord song from their repertoire, to write out the melody in both pentachord versions, and to hum one of them to a partner who decides whether the version is doh or lah pentachord.

EXTENSION ▶

36 **d** ☆ Choral file 9: 'Hush-a-by, my little babe'

Both parts use the lah pentachord on D. The Swedish melody will already be familiar (Pupil's Book 3, page 42).

Skill/Concept
---

37 For a story: building song

▷ On page 48 the children are given the final episode of the dramatic series (Pupil's Book 3, pages 14, 25, 40 and 48) which can remain in simple episodes, or can be combined to make a musical play 'The Ugsome Thing' (see Copymasters – pages 250–254 – for text). The teacher is reminded that suggestions regarding composing and its part in musical plays were given on page 11 of this Teacher's Book ('The place of music in everyday life').

Suggested song
---

20 My old hammer

Music activities

KEY ▶   **37** **a**   From the children's known repertoire recall songs which can be classed as work songs, i.e. songs sung while working and as an aid to work. For example, from the **Key Stage 2A** Song collection:

'Hammering here' (song 33)
'Hill an' gully ride-a' (song 49)

and from the **Key Stage 2B** Song collection:

'My old hammer' (song 20)

Discuss with the children the type of work envisaged by each of the songs. Perform several of them with work actions and at a tempo appropriate to the type of activity.

☆ Pupil's Book 3, page 48   **37** **b**   The children should have sung the 'Building song' with a partner before requesting an analysis chart. The chart has to be completed before they embark on composing a melody for the new words.

37 **c**   Discuss with the children whether this episode is to be linked to 'The Ugsome Thing' story or to be developed as another musical play or to remain as a single dramatic episode.

EXTENSION ▶   **37** **d**   **(i)** Plan an entertainment to take to a retired persons' community club or residential home.

          (ii) Find several elderly neighbours and ask the children to invite them to a musical event such as a class concert, musical play or class assembly.

Towards musical independence

In view of the children's age and considerable experience the teacher will be aware that they are becoming more self-reliant and able to take decisions based on knowledge and skills. The teacher's role has become increasingly reactive to the learning situation and needs of the individual. The Teacher's Book format will reflect this trend and the course will be increasingly 'driven' by the contents of the Pupil's Book and the children's own individual initiatives.

Guidance and pointers will still be given in the Teacher's Book pages, but these will tend to be of a more general nature. Periodic reminders and new teaching ideas will continue to help the teacher in maintaining the children's developing aural, performing, improvising, reading and writing skills. It is assumed by this stage, therefore, that teachers will have developed the teaching patterns which ensure a continual review and reinforcement of the children's skills and, in addition, will want to research and resource at least some of their own materials and teaching ideas.

Skill/Concept

38 The half-bar entry

▷ In song, the natural stresses within the text of the languages used will largely determine the rhythmic characteristics of the melody and the consequent placing of strong and weak beats felt within each phrase. There are many examples where French songs begin a melodic phrase with two weak beats followed by a strong beat in simple time and one weak beat followed by a strong beat in compound time (§). This half-bar start to melodic phrases can be said to be a mark of French folksong style.

It is worth explaining and demonstrating to the children that features of style also occur in a country's national dress and dance.

Suggested songs

4   Cadet Rouselle
7   Di didl lan dan
17   J'ai du bon tabac
20   My old hammer

Music activities

KEY ▶

38 **a**   ☆ Pupil's Book 4, pages 1 and 2

38 **b**   The song 'Cadet Rouselle' has a half-bar entry in §

38 **c**   ☆ Orchestral file 4: 'J'ai du bon tabac'

> **Note:** 'DS al Fine' (*Dal Segno al Fine*) – is an instruction to: 'Go back to the sign and repeat to the end'. Also, note the bars of rest which appear in Parts A and B.

COURSE PROGRAMME

Skill/Concept

39 Music for the dance

▷ Continuing with the theme of style in French traditional music, the children are presented with a dance melody from Provence called the Farandole.

Music activities

KEY ▶

☆ Pupil's Book 4, page 3

39 a

The Farandole

This dance is traditional to the Provence region of southern France. It was probably introduced there by the Phoenicians whose version was similar to a dance of the Ancient Greeks.

It is essentially an outdoor chain dance. Men and women alternately form a long line linked by hands. The leader takes the dancers through a number of figures which have names to indicate the winding evolutions of the dance – the Snail, the Bridges, the Maze. One of the principal figures is passing the chain beneath an arc formed by the raised arms of a couple in the chain and then back through again. The steps are introduced at various times by the leader. Generally speaking the chain moves with long and rapid steps. However, more intricate steps include 'le pas Nicois' – one leg crossed over the other at knee height, first in front, then behind; 'le pas Arlesein' – one foot crossed over the other, the toe touching the ground. Jumps and turns take place, the last jump being as high as possible.

The Farandole has much in common with the Cornish furry dance.

39 b If the music is available on disc the children can listen to the well-known farandole from Bizet's music for Daudet's play 'L'Arlésienne'. Interestingly, although the melody is traditional it uses a $\frac{2}{4}$ metre rather than the more usual $\frac{6}{8}$.

Skill/Concept

40 ### The hexachord on lah. The semitone

▷ Pupil's Book 4, pages 4 and 5 introduce the lah hexachord and the concept of the semitone. It will be important for the children to aurally recognise and appreciate the significance of the semitone – which is an important feature of melody using notes of the lah and doh pentachords/ hexachords and, later in the children's experience, scale structures, keys and modulations.

A keyboard with a black and white note layout is extremely desirable when introducing the semitone concept.

Music activities

KEY ▶

40 **a** ☆ **Reading Sheet 15B**

Ask the children to sing through the melody to solfa. Aurally it feels like a lah pentachord melody because the new note (me-fah) occurs only in the penultimate bar. When the melody is secured by using solfa, ask the children to sing with the words.

40 **b** Referring to the keyboard, introduce the concept of the semitone. Explain that semitones occur between adjacent notes, whatever the colour (white or black). Therefore, when using white notes only (as we have been so far), the semitones occur between B and C, and E and F. The note at the top of the hexachord in Reading Sheet 15B (F) is therefore a semitone higher than E.

Still working with the keyboard, it will be possible to deduce that when the children have sung me-fah in doh pentachordal/hexachordal melodies they have sung semitones; similarly, they have sung semitones when they have sung te-doh in D-lah and A-lah pentachordal melodies. NB: The lah hexachord contains both semitones, te-doh and me-fah.

40 **c** Ask the children to sing: **d–r**, **r–m** and then **m–f**. Can they hear the larger step of pitch between **d–r** (and **r–m**) and the smaller step, **m–f**? Several repeats of the note series may be helpful, with the children employing handsigns. Explain to the children that the smaller step is known as an interval of a semitone and the larger step, a tone.

The semitone of te–doh can be felt when singing the lah pentachord (l,–t,–d–r–m). Ask the children to sing from handsigns the note series l,–t, t,–d d–r r–m and to detect the semitone (t,–d) without previously informing them.

☆ **Pupil's Book 4, pages 4 and 5**

40 **d** At this stage, confine the children to lah = A when using a keyboard.

☆ **Pupil's Book 4, page 6**

40 **e** On page 6 of Pupil's Book 4, the children are encouraged to use the lah hexachord formula when lah = D and G. In this way, they discover the necessity to use flat notes in order to conform to the pattern of tones and semitones.

Skill/Concept

41 The lah hexachord on D. The flat (♭)

▷ The song 'One for each night' (page 7 of Pupil's Book 4) celebrates the Jewish festival of Hanukkah, or the Festival of Lights, which occurs in December and commemorates the victory of the Jews over King Antiochus in 165BC and the restoration of the Temple in Jerusalem. As Barbara Cass-Beggs explains in her excellent book *A Musical Calendar of Festivals* (Ward Lock Educational): 'When the temple's lamp was lit, it was said to have burned for eight days even though there was only enough oil to keep it alight for one day. This miracle is remembered in Jewish homes today when a new candle is placed in the menorah (a special candlestick) on each evening of Hanukkah, until on the last evening there are eight candles burning.'

Other traditions also have an annual festival in which light has a significant meaning. Divali is the Hindu festival of lights celebrating the New Year and the goddess of prosperity. Sikhs keep the festival in memory of their sixth Guru, Hargobind. Sweden traditionally celebrated the festival of Saint Lucia with a girl chosen to wear a crown of lighted candles, a white dress and a scarlet sash. She visited the country farms and houses and promised the inhabitants good fortune and prosperity.

An aural perception of the semitones between **m–f** and **t–d** (see Pupil's Book 4, page 6) enables the children to hear the necessity to make certain keyboard notes conform to the hexachord patterns of tones and semitones by playing a black note rather than its white letter name equivalent. For example, for the lah hexachord on D:

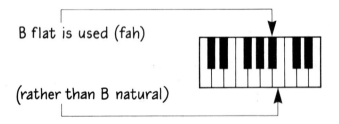

B flat is used (fah)

(rather than B natural)

Consequently, it is necessary to show this on the staff by preceding the affected note (or notes) with a flat sign (♭).

Music activities

KEY ▶

41 a Invite children to improvise melodies on keyboard instruments with the lah hexachord on D.

41 b Ask a child to improvise a melodic phrase to solfa using notes of the lah hexachord on D. The class repeat the phrase singing to fixed pitch names. B flat should be sung as 'bes' (pronounced 'bez').

☆ **Pupil's Book 4,**
  page 7

41 **c** **(i)** As a feature of musical style it is interesting to note that there are many examples of melody in the Jewish tradition which use a lah-based tonality including the lah pentachord and hexachord. Reading Sheet 16A is an Israeli pioneering song, 'Oh the young man works on the lands'. The verse melody uses notes of the lah pentachord, while the chorus uses **d–t,–l,–m,**.

☆ **Reading Sheet 16A**

At this stage (Pupil's Book 4, pages 7 to 12), the B flat is written against the note B each time it occurs.

(ii) First and second time bars are a useful convention for saving both writing time and space on the page. The children may care to remember this device when writing their own music.

41 **d** ☆ **Choral file 10: 'Little Johnny dances'**

Skill/Concept

42 **The doh hexachord on F**

▷ Melodies based on the doh pentachord/hexachord on F require the use
of B flat.

Music activities

KEY ▶
☆ **Pupil's Book 4,**
  page 8

42 **a** The two-part arrangement of the Flemish folksong incorporates the use of
low 'te' (lower part, penultimate note). Although quite a short piece, the
arrangement contains a number of interesting features of construction with
which the children will be familiar, e.g. anacrusis, repeat marks,
sequence, tied notes, first and second time bars.

42 **b** As the class sings a drone (a continuously sustained note) to the vowel 'ah'
on note F, an individual child improvises a melody on the F doh hexachord
by singing to fixed pitch names or by playing on a keyboard instrument.

Skill/Concept

43 The tonalities of doh and lah hexachords

▷ The children are now familiar with using doh and lah hexachords. Both hexachords have four notes in common (**f m r d**) but their different tone and semitone formulae give each a very distinctive aural character. Earlier work with doh and lah pentatones sought to draw out the individual qualities of doh- and lah-based melodies.

Changing between doh- and lah-based tone-sets within a melody produces a musical effect which is of considerable expressive and structural significance.

Music activities

KEY ▶
☆ Pupil's Book 4, page 9

43 a The English folk dance 'Temple Barr' exemplifies a melodic feature common to music of varying styles and origins. The notes of bars 1–4 are drawn from the lah pentachord, whereas those for bars 5–7 are notes of the doh hexachord on F. Finally, the music returns to the lah pentachord section.

43 b Dictation. Invent suitable short phrases, using the doh hexachord on F and the lah hexachord on D. The children write in staff notation, inserting the flat sign (♭) as appropriate.

Skill/Concept

44 **Recognising tonality and using tonality in composing**

▷ Recognising, identifying and using different tonalities in improvising, reading and composing music greatly adds to the children's awareness and understanding of form and structure in longer pieces.

Tonality also plays an important role as an expressive element in music, and contributes significantly to the character of the music, its mood and its energy.

Composing requires a feeling for tonality – a sense of relationship between notes and groups of notes. On page 11 of Pupil's Book 4 the children are concerned only with the so-called 'major tonality' of the doh-based tone-set and the 'minor tonality' of the lah-based tone-set.

Music activities

KEY ▶

☆ Pupil's Book 4,
  pages 10 and 11

 44 a Working in pairs, the children sing known songs to each other with the object of determining whether each example is doh (major) or lah (minor) based; they list their decisions and compare these with those made by the other children of the class. It may be helpful for one partner to hum a drone on lah or doh (according to the tonality) as a way of helping the decision making.

EXTENSION ▶

 44 b Material from other sources which have strong tonalities alternating between major and minor might suggest themselves. For example, recorded music such as the Polovtsian Dances ('Prince Igor') by Borodin and the well-known 'Song of the Volga boatmen'.

44 c ☆ Orchestral file 5: 'Oh Susannah'

Skill/Concept

45 For an occasion: ceremonial march

▷ The purpose of marching music is well understood by children. However, they are not always aware that there is a diversity of occasion when marches are required. Regimental marches are used for brisk military march pasts; slow marches are needed for solemn occasions, e.g. the annual Remembrance Day ceremonies; marches for a specific function such as a film (e.g. 'The Dambusters March' by Eric Coates) or a state ceremony (e.g. the Coronation March 'Crown Imperial' by William Walton).

Marches can be written for a variety of instrumental combinations, from the military fife with drum to the full military band or orchestra. If brass instruments are not available, fanfares played on recorders can be quite effective, or brass voices on a keyboard if available. The children may decide on more successful alternatives.

Music activities

KEY ▶

45 **a** Listen to a recorded or live example of a march. Discuss with the children the purpose of the march and its musical make-up, e.g. structure, dynamics, tempo, time signature, rhythm and melodic elements, instruments.

The marches of Philip Sousa will provide a rich source of listening.

45 **b** The children would be interested to hear recorded (or live) examples of fanfares, including those for a single instrument. Broadcasts of events at which Royalty is present, and State occasions, such as the Opening of Parliament, will provide excellent opportunities for the children to hear fanfares. In addition, bugle calls, which are musically not unlike fanfares but have a rather different intention, can be heard at ceremonies such as a Remembrance Day observance and the so-called 'Beating the retreat' by a military band.

☆ Pupil's Book 4, pages 12 and 13

EXTENSION ▶

45 **c** It could be appropriate at this stage to introduce the concept of the trumpet as a transposing instrument, if the instrument is available for illustration. Because of the build of the instrument it is necessary to write the notes on the staff one tone higher than those it is required to sound, e.g **s–m–d** written as G doh will actually sound **s–m–d** in F doh. An understanding of this concept will be essential when a transposing instrument (e.g. trumpet, clarinet, horn) is to play simultaneously with a non-transposing instrument.

Skill/Concept

---

46   **The key signature**

▷ The key signature saves the necessity of writing flat or sharp symbols before every appearance of the affected note. It is then assumed that the affected notes are altered accordingly throughout the piece.

Please avoid using the phrase 'the key of F major' when referring, for example, to a melody using the F doh hexachord; melodies should not be designated as being only major or minor. Many melodies are best categorised according to the sort of labels which have occurred in the course, e.g. lah pentachord, soh pentatone etc. Accurate descriptions of the pitch structure of melodies will support the children's learning process and help avoid confusion.

Music activities

KEY ▶

☆ Pupil's Book 4,
   pages 14 and 15

46 a   **(i)** 'Coulter's Candy' uses the dotted rhythm pattern of ♩. ♪ and ♪ ♩. The latter pattern, together with similar shorter patterns such as ♫. , typifies much Scottish traditional music and in its quicker form is generally referred to as 'the snap'. Refer the children to other Scottish melodies contained in the Song collection.

         (ii) Remind the children of the song 'I saw three ships' (Reading Sheet 12).

         ☆ **Reading Sheet 12**

46 b   ☆ **Choral file 11: 'Coulter's Candy'**

EXTENSION ▶   **46** c   ☆ **Choral file 13: 'Coulter's Candy'**

Skill/Concept

47 Working with the doh hexachord on F

▷ Today we have a fairly restricted use for the word carol, usually a song or hymn sung at Christmas time. In fact, the early carols (13th–15th centuries) were often danced, probably as round dances, as well as sung. The carol has in the past been a song to celebrate any religious festival, or season of the year, or an important occasion or event (e.g. the Agincourt Carol was composed to celebrate the English victory at the battle of Agincourt in 1415).

The traditional carol can be identified by the dance lilt quality of its compound rhythm, the simplicity of its text and melody (it usually had its origins among people of humble literary and musical skills) and the directness of thought and expression.

The Christmas carols of France are called noëls (noël = Christmas). The word has survived in English as 'nowell', sometimes found as the refrain of a carol.

Music activities

KEY ▶
☆ Pupil's Book 4, pages 16 and 17

47 a With the children, compile a list of known Christmas carols. Through performance and researching information from carol books and hymn books, estimate the period and region of origin. How many carols originate from other countries? Which carol is the oldest? What features do the examples show? How many carols have a triple simple time metre, or a compound time metre? How many have a verse and refrain structure? Are there examples that have a dance lilt or jig-like feel to them?

47 b Can any known songs sung at other seasons or occasions (e.g. harvest festival) be identified as carols? The *Oxford Book of Carols* will provide suitable examples for the children to learn, as will the excellent volumes *A Musical Calendar of Festivals*, chosen by Barbara Cass-Beggs (published by Ward Lock Educational) and *Light the Candles!* by June B Tillman (Cambridge University Press).

EXTENSION ▶

47 c Some children may wish to write a carol to celebrate a different season of the year or a special occasion other than Christmas (e.g. the opening of new buildings).

47 d ☆ Orchestral file 6: 'I saw three ships'

Skill/Concept

48 ## At the disco

▷ Children are aware of the style of music used at discos and with the general culture of 'pop' music. Much of the musical style depends on sophisticated electronics, capable 'backing' performers and engineers. As a result, the musical content can sound complex and difficult to imitate. Although lacking the means to make the style totally convincing, most children will accept limitations of equipment and expertise and will strive enthusiastically for some of the essential qualities of 'pop' music that they have access to and can control.

Music activities

KEY ▶

48 **a** Listen to an example of a recorded 'pop' song, one that has an important melodic vocal line, is accessible to the children and their vocal capability, and is not esoteric. Examine the following aspects in your selected example:

- rhythm – ask the children to tap the pulse as they listen to the example. Select a vocal phrase or two for the children to hear and sing several times so they can assimilate the rhythm. Ask them to tap the rhythm of the phrase(s) with one hand as the other hand maintains a steady pulse.
- melody – are there points of melodic interest that characterise the vocal and melodic style of 'pop' songs?
- structure – ask the children to comment on the phrase structure of the melody? How many distinctive phrases were the children aware of? Did repetition and sequence feature?

☆ Pupil's Book 4,
pages 18 and 19

EXTENSION ▶

48 **b** It is quite possible that, with their enthusiasm to develop the given song or their own compositions, children will wish to employ the assistance of several performers. They may want to record the song on audio or visual tape and use amplification for performing.

48 **c** **U69–U71** are melodic examples to read from the board. Alternatively, they may be used for dictation. For dictation purposes allow the children to hear an example sung to 'la' several times, then to perform to a tapped pulse and to memorise before attempting to write in rhythm-solfa notation. If necessary, work with one phrase at a time. Some children might write the rhythm only. As another option the rhythm might be given on the board and the children (working collectively, or in pairs or individually) add the solfa.

Skill/Concept

49 Working with canons

▷ European church music between 1200 and 1600 is invariably of several melodic parts and usually described as being polyphonic in style. But music, especially vocal music of all ages and within a variety of cultures has always retained an interest in the polyphonic style. A practical understanding of the style is still considered to be a useful part of the improviser's, the composer's and the choral singer's craft today.

Two-part examples in the Key Stage 2 Course often reflect the polyphonic style, e.g. Reading Sheets 16B, 17B, 18 and 19B

Music activities

KEY ▶
☆ Pupil's Book 4,
  pages 20 and 21

49 **a** Draw the children's attention to the parts being confined to notes of the doh hexachord + t,. The music is an extract from a longer piece by Josquin des Prés.

Encourage a variety of performances to take place using groups, large and small, and in duet. Children performing in duet and small groups should first experiment with various performing considerations relating to tempo, dynamics, breathing and vocal style.

49 **b** Try to arrange for the children to hear examples of polyphonic music, preferably in a setting and acoustic for which the music was intended. The canon by Mozart moves melodically by step, apart from the interval t,–f in the upper part. This will need preparatory attention with the help of handsigns.

49 **c** Listen to examples on disc, at a concert or church service of choral music for several singing parts, e.g. the church music of Byrd, Bach, Handel, Haydn and Mozart.

Skill/Concept

50 The doh hexachord on D. The sharp (♯)

▷ Where there are children, games of their own invention are played. Games are the natural products of children's minds in social circumstances. In these games there is much that is universally shared among children, so that one type of game can be found in local versions in many countries.

Children's singing games have been a rich source of material to include in *Growing with Music* Song collections. The music of children's games is a spontaneous outcome of children's thinking, retaining its freshness and appeal to each succeeding generation, and therefore providing an obvious category of material to be included in any collection for children's use.

The children are introduced to the sharp sign, which has the effect of raising the note by a semitone. F sharp will be an essential note to the doh hexachord on D, and, at this stage, for the purposes of notation, the sharp sign will be placed in the first space. The convention of positioning the F sharp sign on the fifth line is reserved for the major and minor key signatures, G major and E minor, which occur later.

Music activities

KEY ▶

50 **a** Ask the children to sing a known doh hexachord song and then for individuals to play the melody on a keyboard several times with doh = G; C; F. What happens when doh = D? Explain that note F is altered upwards (not G downwards) and show this on the board as follows:

Point out that the semitone between me and fah is thus retained. Sing the doh hexachord on D up and down to fixed pitch names. F sharp should be sung as 'fis' (pronounced 'feece').

50 **b** Ask a child to improvise a melodic fragment (3 or 4 notes) on a keyboard or pitched percussion instrument using notes of the doh hexachord on D. A second child extends the fragment into a full-length phrase. This is repeated by the class singing to solfa, and then to fixed pitch names.

☆ Pupil's Book 4, page 22

50 **c** The Zulu stone game is one of many similar games played by children throughout the world. For the game each child has a similar object, such as a bean bag, a stick of a suitable size – stones could be used if the game is played out-of-doors. Everyone kneels in a circle. The stone is placed in front of the knees. Working to the pulse, each person simultaneously picks up the stone of the right-hand neighbour and places it in front as before. The sequence is repeated. Also compare the Ghanaian version of the game, 'Obwisana' (song 62 in the **Key Stage 2A** Song collection).

☆ Pupil's Book 4,
    page 23

50 **d**   As part of the children's efforts to devise their own games it would be helpful to categorise known games and analyse why particular games are successful.

EXTENSION ▶   **50** **e**   ☆ **Orchestral file 7: 'Country dance'**

This lively piece is based entirely on notes of the doh pentachord on D.

> Careful and detailed research of children's games with copious illustrations can be found in the books of Iona and Peter Opie, e.g. *The Singing Game, Children's Games in Street and Playground* and *The Lore and Language of Schoolchildren*, all published by OUP.

Skill/Concept

| 51 | Composing: doh hexachord on D

▷ Setting words to music, or setting music to words? There are a variety of ways of creating songs. Sometimes both words and music are a product of a tandem creative process. The children's page presents words for setting to music.

Environmental issues have become increasingly thought about and discussed. It is right that children should be concerned with the debate about matters which affect their lives directly.

Many songs are associated with a cause or concern, e.g. 'Where have all the flowers gone?' – an anti-war song; 'Come home, father' – against the abuse of alcohol; 'We are the world' – concern for the victims of famine (a song by Michael Jackson and Lionel Ritchie).

Songs about causes, sung by the children, performed by a visiting singer, or listened to as recorded music, could initiate interesting discussion about such songs. Indeed such songs, including those composed by the class, could form part of a topic. The beachcomber songs could start an environmental topic involving the whole school.

Music activities

KEY▶

☆ Pupil's Book 4, page 24

| 51 | **a** The creative process during composing is essentially a personal activity involving the judgement and decision making of the individual alone. Therefore, children will need time on their own to contemplate the words. Some will work with the procedure given on the pupil's page; while others can be encouraged to improvise melodically straight away, experimenting, changing and refining both the rhythm and pitch content as they proceed.

For their composing it is essential that children should feel confident with the procedure they adopt, and above all, they need to work with an 'inner ear' that can produce sound internally and is processed through channels of musical thinking, experience and knowledge.

| 51 | **b** ☆ Reading Sheet 16B

This is a canon in two parts which becomes a four-part canon when each part is performed in canon with itself.

☆ Pupil's Book 4, page 25

| 51 | **c** This version of 'Shepherd's Hey', the well-known folk dance melody, uses the doh pentachord on D.

EXTENSION▶

| 51 | **d** ☆ Orchestral file 8: 'Drops of brandy'

This is an arrangement of an English folk dance melody. Bring the $\frac{9}{8}$ time signature to the children's attention – 3 beats to the bar using compound time rhythms.

The melody may be easier to read if presented as a doh pentachord + **d'**. It is suitable for a good recorder player to play.

Skill/Concept

52 Lah hexachord on E

▷ Page 26 of Pupil's Book 4 has a traditional Serbian melody based on notes of the lah hexachord. The country of Serbia existed as part of the Austro-Hungarian Empire until the end of the First World War. There is a large Serbian population in south-eastern Europe and their traditional culture is very much alive.

Musical activities

KEY ▶

52 a Work with previous teaching ideas to establish the children's aural understanding of the lah hexachord on E. It will be helpful to use examples from known music and to improvise in solfa and to fixed pitch names (F sharp should be sung as 'fis') with appropriate keyboard illustrations.

52 b Examples of staff notation will require the key signature of F sharp, which should still be placed in the first space of the staff at this stage.

☆ Pupil's Book 4, pages 26 and 27

52 c Draw the children's attention to the presence of ♩. ♪ in bar 5 of 'The Serbian song' and allow them to practise it by tapping the phrase which contains this rhythm. This dotted rhythm should also become an identifiable feature of the children's improvising and writing.

EXTENSION ▶

52 d Discuss with the children the factors that help to identify a culture, e.g. language; customs; religions; the arts. What part does music play in establishing the identity of the culture? Are children aware of their own traditions and cultural background? Are children aware of important facets in other traditions and cultures?

Skill/Concept

---

53 Structure: changing tonalities

▷ Changing tonality is frequently used as a device to support longer structures. Comparisons can be made between longer structures – a play has acts and scenes, a novel has chapters, a poem has verses, a symphony has sections and movements. All these structures are held together by a succession of ideas within a framework of real time. The framework of time and the use of memory correlates successive ideas into a meaningful structure. Unrelated ideas, ideas that do not reappear or inform other ideas, and an imbalance between ideas and time-length usually result in a poorly structured piece – unmemorable and dissatisfying in its effect on the listener, reader or performer.

A section of music can be recognised by the sum of its component parts – rhythm, pitch, phrase lengths, dynamics, etc. One of the dimensions of pitch is tonality – the product of a recurring group of notes (tone-set) which can usually be labelled, e.g. doh hexachord on D. The same tonality in successive phrases has a unifying effect and helps to stamp an identity on that section; a new tonality helps to establish the identity of a new section.

Music can touch all our senses and conjure up all our moods. But music which leaves us without a feeling of having experienced a 'journey', of having 'travelled and arrived', is probably music without shape or form – the memory cannot remember and the emotions are left untouched.

Music activities

KEY ▶
☆ Pupil's Book 4, page 28

53 a The structural plan provided on pupil's page 28 serves as an example. Some children may wish to plan more extended and complex structures; they should be encouraged to do this and to review the results critically through performance.

Planning is important in longer structures. However, planning should always be musically conceived and in this the children's previous experience, knowledge and 'inner hearing' ability will be important. Planning should not stultify the spontaneous instinct. Music exists and lives when its sound is being conceived and performed. Experience, knowledge and the 'inner ear' produce the plan, but performing should be allowed to alter and refine the plan.

53 b ☆ Reading Sheet 17A

Reading Sheet 17A, for reading in 2 parts, is based on the song 'Willum he had seven sons'. Sing to solfa and then fixed pitch names. A performance on two instruments of contrasting timbre could be attempted.

EXTENSION ▶ | 53 | **c**   ☆ Reading Sheet 17B

Example 17B is two-part music constructed with many delayed notes. Delayed notes are used here for the device of 'suspension and resolution'. The principle is that one part suspends its current note as the other part moves to a new note. In this example, the suspended note is resolved downwards by step after one beat. Suspensions and resolutions occur frequently in each part.

Perform the piece at varying tempos asking the children for their observations.

| 53 | **d**   ☆ **Choral file 12: 'Apple Tree'**

The doh hexachord melody is graphically supported by an inventive second part.

| 53 | **e**   **Melody dominoes** ☆ Worksheets 4–7 (pages 168–172)

Worksheet 4: Preparations
Worksheet 5: Rules for the game
Worksheet 6/7: The melody dominoes
Worksheet 8: Score sheet

This game will prove to be challenging and popular with the children. The 'Preparations' and 'Rules for the Game' sheets need to be read and understood first by the teacher. The dominoes should be mounted on suitable card for the purposes of better wear and ease of handling.

Skill/Concept

54 Syncopation

▷ The music of some traditions is rich in the use of syncopated rhythm. It is particularly so with the music of the Caribbean, Africa, Eastern Europe and the USA, but syncopation features to a greater or lesser degree in most countries.

Syncopation may be defined as melodic or purely rhythmic note stresses that do not occur simultaneously with the pulse. The sophisticated use of syncopation is essential to certain styles of music – jazz, bigband, rock – in which rhythm phrase and accent frequently anticipates or avoids the beat.

Syncopation will be an established part of the children's aural experience through those songs containing syncopation in the **Key Stage 2** Song collections, and through familiarity with music on radio, television and tapes. However, all styles of music have incidences of rhythm syncopation, including classical music, e.g. the music of Stravinsky, and folk music across the world.

Suggested songs

8   Four white horses
10   Go dung a Manuel Road
29   Right tru, right tru, de rocky road

Music activities

KEY ▶

54 **a**   Sing songs from the Song collections which contain rhythm syncopation, e.g. from the **Key Stage 2B** Song collection (listed above) and from the **Key Stage 2A** collection:

80   Hey Johnny
91   Oh, won't you sit down?
110   Alice the camel (see Pupil's Book 4, page 29)
119   La, la (Artsa alina)

(i) As a song is sung the children tap a steady pulse.

(ii) Ask a group to tap a steady pulse as a second group tap the rhythm of a song.

(iii) Perform the rhythm of a song with one child playing a steady pulse on a tambour and another playing a tapped rhythm, as the class listen.

(iv) The children perform a song maintaining a tapped pulse with one hand and the rhythm with the other.

With these suggested activities encourage the children to be aware of those rhythms whose movement does not occur simultaneously with the beats and to observe the off-beat accents which result.

54 **b** **U72–U73** provide written examples for children to read from the board: **a** is written without syncopation; **b** re-written to include syncopated rhythms (the use of tied notes and delayed notes is already familiar to the children); **c** shows the syncopated rhythms written in conventional notation.

U74–U77 are syncopated rhythms for the children to read from the board. A steady and audible pulse will be needed at all times. Syncopated rhythms have a momentum – take care to choose a tempo which is neither too slow nor too fast.

In the following examples the $\frac{2}{2}$ time signature is used. The beat is now a half note (minim).

Beats:

It is suggested that these examples are performed in a variety of ways, e.g. with consecutive performances with varied tempos and dynamics. They could also be performed in canon. But on all occasions a steady pulse should be felt by each child.

☆ Pupil's Book 4, page 29

54 c Rhythm phrases containing syncopation from known songs could be identified and written down. Refer back to the disco melody (Pupil's Book 4, page 18).

54 d Encourage children to improvise rhythms containing syncopation as:

- an ostinato accompaniment to a song;
- a second part to a written rhythm piece.

☆ Pupil's Book 4, page 30

54 e This is a lively Irish sea-song with a real sense of relief and joy for the seaman who has been away from home for possibly many months.

EXTENSION ▶

54 f ☆ Reading Sheet 18

Preparation time spent on obtaining accuracy with the syncopated rhythms, especially ♩. ♩. ♩ will be rewarded in performance of the piece. For example, practise the following:

These examples of accented syncopation are features of Caribbean music. Draw the children's attention to the way the melody changes part and its use of the doh hexachord on F. The accompaniment part uses a wider tone-set.

Perform the piece with voices and with instruments.

54 **g** Listen to recorded music containing syncopated rhythms, e.g. the songs 'Gee, Officer Krupke' and 'Something's coming' from the musical 'West Side Story' (Bernstein and Sondheim).

54 **h** ☆ **Reading Sheet 19A**

This Reading Sheet is for performing on instruments. It contains two types of syncopation: (i) the missed beat, and (ii) tied notes. The piece is reminiscent of East European traditional music. When the piece is sufficiently known it could be performed with a steady but constant accelerando until a furious pace has been achieved! Chords have been given for guitar or improvised piano accompaniment.

> All styles of music employ syncopation to lesser or greater degrees. The jazz piano playing of Oscar Petersen features sophisticated and complex syncopation, while the music of, say, Mozart, Beethoven and Tschaikovsky use syncopation in a more contained way. The 'Scotch snap' is a simple instance of syncopation and a typical feature of Scottish folk music. Syncopation is rare in the English tradition but is a common feature in the dance music of Eastern Europe.
>
> However, it is the 20th century which has seen a development of syncopation in music and this is largely due to the influence of the folk music of Africa and South America. Most popular music uses syncopated rhythm and composers such as Stravinsky, Milhaud and Poulenc have employed elements of jazz and popular music styles, particularly music they wrote during the 1920s–1940s, e.g. 'Ebony Concerto' by Stravinsky; 'La Creation du Monde' by Milhaud.

54 **i** ☆ **Orchestral file 9: 'Russian dance'**

This arrangement features syncopated rhythms which use the eighth note rest and tied notes. The melody is from Reading Sheet 19A. The third part maintains a steady pulse throughout.

Skill/Concept

55 ## Composing with syncopation

▷ The children are likely to be familiar with Caribbean styles of music from radio, television, records, or from having heard or played in a steel band. Any experience should be supplemented by further opportunities to listen to traditional and modern Caribbean styles – calypso, mento, ska, reggae. Invite performing musicians to the school.

The opportunity should not be missed to familiarise children with important aspects of the Caribbean – the geography, history and culture. Materials and helpful literature can be obtained from the following addresses:

WOMAD (World of Music and Dance)
Mill Lane
Box
Wiltshire   SN14 9PN

Knock on Wood
Unit 1
30 Dock Street
Leeds   LS10 1JF

The Multi-cultural Education Service
The Teacher's Centre
Birches Barn Road
Penn Fields
Wolverhampton   WV3 7BJ

The Commonwealth Institute
Educational Resource Centre
Kensington High Street
London   W8 6NQ

It is most important that the children improvise regularly with syncopation of the kind used in Caribbean music, and against a strongly felt pulse, until they have an instinctive and spontaneous feel for these rhythms. It is undesirable for children to study syncopation largely from the written symbol.

Music activities

KEY ▶

☆ Pupil's Book 4, page 31

55 a   ☆ Reading Sheet 19B

This piece reflects the calypso style of Caribbean music, and can be sung and/or played on instruments. If it is sung the children should first sing to solfa before performing with agreed wordless sounds, e.g. da-dee; du-bee; la. The top part (first part) uses the doh hexachord + **t,**; the lower part (second part) has the tone-set **f m r d t, l, s,** + **ta,**. Appropriate rhythms played sensitively on instruments such as bongoes, congas, claves and agogo would provide an accompaniment to enhance the performance, e.g.

☆ Pupil's Book 4, page 32

55 b   *Mango Spice* – 44 Caribbean songs chosen by Conolly, Cameron and Singham (published by A & C Black, 1981) is an excellent collection of songs with helpful background information and advice.

55 **c** ☆ Orchestral file 10: 'Shepherd's Hey'

This uses the well-known folk melody 'Shepherd's Hey' (Pupil's Book 4, page 25) and is a good example of the English tradition which does not feature syncopation. It is a three-part arrangement for instruments, but could be performed chorally. It could also be played on recorders.

55 **d** ☆ Choral file 13: 'Coulter's Candy'

This version adds a third part to the arrangement in Choral file 11.

Skill/Concept

56 The Natural Minor scale on E

▷ The children's pitch experience is summarised below and shows the principle tone-sets they have encountered.

doh pentatone	**d–r–m–s–l–d'**
lah pentatone	**l,–d–r–m–s–l**
soh pentatone	**s,–l,–d–r–m–s**

doh tetrachord	**d–r–m–f**
doh pentachord	**d–r–m–f–s**
doh hexachord	**d–r–m–f–s–l**
lah pentachord	**l,–t,–d–r–m**
lah hexachord	**l,–t,–d–r–m–f**

At this stage, our first diatonic scale is introduced; a diatonic scale is a series of eight notes adjacent to each other, consisting of tones and semitones.

Most scales have acquired universally agreed names, e.g. the Natural Minor scale. By extending the lah hexachord to include 'soh' we arrive at the Natural Minor. The Natural Minor scale is formed by adding lah as the final note thus:

ascending **l,–t,–d–r–m–f–s–l** and
descending **l–s–f–m–r–d–t,–l,**

Music activities

KEY ▶

56 **a** With the involvement of the children, find, sing and list one song example for each of the above tone-sets.

56 **b** In imitation of the teacher the children should first sing to solfa the Natural Minor scale on E (**l,–t,–d–r–m–f–s–l**) ascending and descending, with the support of handsigns, then to fixed pitch names – E F ♯ ('Feece') G A B C D E.

56 **c** Now ask the children to perform the scale in similar ways, but to selected rhythms. For example:

Explain to the children the meaning of the word 'diatonic' – 'containing tones and semitones'. The Natural Minor scale is a diatonic scale. Point out, therefore, that pentatones are not diatonic because they contain no semitone intervals.

☆ **Pupil's Book 4, page 33**

EXTENSION ▶

56 **d** Ask the children to build melodies on the two bars given, choosing from the blocks below:

(i) an 8-bar melody which changes tonality
(ii) an 8-bar melody which keeps to the Natural Minor.

The children may wish to build longer melodies in a similar way. They could make building blocks of their own.

Skill/Concept

57   The Natural Minor scale on D

▷ When working with page 34 of Pupil's Book 4, if instruments are in short supply, simple instruments such as kazoos can be used to supplement the classroom orchestra.

When working with page 35 of Pupil's Book 4, the children's wide experience of performing song melody will give them an adequate basis for making a reasoned choice for their two bars. The children are asked to fill the missing section by choosing a suitable block, and to use a style which is suitable for a Russian song. Even in such a vast region as Russia there are regional stylistic traits to be found. Much of the traditional music of this country shows recurring characteristics. For example:

- the use of the Natural Minor or lah-based tonalities;
- the strong sense of pulse;
- the repetitive use of syncopated rhythmic fragments (ti-ta-ti);
- the frequency of the falling melodic intervals of the fifth and fourth (also the rising fourth), in particular, **l–m/m–l,**.

Many dances of the region have the same characteristics as their song counterparts, e.g. the Ukrainian Hopak and the Russian Kohanachka.

Music activities

KEY ▶

☆ **Pupil's Book 4,**
  pages 34 and 35

57 a   ☆ Reading Sheet 20

The children might use this Reading Sheet to make reading cards (in rhythm solfa or staff notation) – one bar per card – for reading in canon. Using two performers, the cards are passed from one to the other and sung by each child in succession. Please note that this Hungarian melody is lah pentachord plus **l,** and **s,** – not the Natural Minor scale.

57 b   The original melody on Pupil's Book 4 page 5 used block 'e' in the missing bars.

Skill/Concept

58 **Styles with the Natural Minor**

▷ Greek music is varied in style, showing the influence of Turkey (Greece was long part of the Turkish empire) and the nearby Balkan countries. The music varies from region to region. Spontaneous embellishment of the melody, including descending melodic slides, by the singer, often results in a decorative and sometimes rhythmically ornate melody, in common with other middle east styles.

English melody, on the other hand, generally has simpler rhythmic features; the melodic pitch used is wider and the melodic line more angular than its Greek counterpart.

Music activities

KEY ▶   **58** **a**   ☆ Pupil's Book 4, pages 36 and 37

EXTENSION ▶   **58** **b**   ☆ Choral file 14: 'Wraggle Taggle Gypsies'

This is a very old Natural Minor English folksong.

58 **c**   ☆ Orchestral file 11: 'Rochdale coconut dance'

The coconut dance is a morris dance particular to Lancashire, England. It is danced by eight men dressed in black breeches and blackened faces. They perform various figures in single file, circles and squares. Essentially, the rhythms are provided by the dancers who beat small domes of wood, like half coconuts, fastened to the palms of hands, knees and waist. With the coconuts on their hands they clap their own and those of their partners. The dance resembles that of Licoco in Provence, France. Notice the change of tonality in the middle section.

Skill/Concept

| 59 | The Natural Minor on A

Music activities

KEY ▶

☆ Pupil's Book 4,
  pages 38 and 39

| 59 | a   The song, 'Pedro, go, go Pescador', is written in the Natural Minor on A. Consequently, it gives the melody a range of notes which do not lie conveniently for the voice. It is suggested that the class could learn the song by rote using the Natural Minor on E.

The analysis of the song is divided into upper and lower boxes – the 'Section' boxes marking the broad divisions of the song, and the 'Structure' boxes showing the repeats within each section. For the task of writing a new version in compound time it would probably be helpful to many children if several bars are first worked on the board before the children continue independently.

Portuguese folksong is abundant and varied, combining African, Spanish and Brazilian melodic rhythmic elements in the 'fado', an urban folksong genre.

Repetition, contrast and similarity are always important ingredients in musical structure. The analysis of the Portuguese melody on the pupil's page shows that there are three distinct sections: A is repeated, and B provides a distinctive, but not dissimilar section. Basically, each section is built on the repetition of a single structural phrase, except that the second-time ending to phrase A is modified (Av(variant)). There is similarity, therefore, between A and Av.

A piece of music with clear A B A sections is traditionally referred to as **ternary form**. A piece with a recurring A section and a new section sandwiched between, e.g. A B A C A, is traditionally referred to as **rondo form**. Many of the solo concertos and sonatas of the late 18th and 19th centuries had a final movement based on a developed version of the rondo form, e.g. the Horn Concerto No. 3 by Mozart.

EXTENSION ▶

| 59 | b   ☆ Orchestral file 12: 'Ukraine melody'

In those sections of the piece which have a minor tonality the use of G sharps is in keeping with the style of the Ukrainian melody.

COURSE PROGRAMME

Skill/Concept

60 The Authentic Major

▷ Many older people remember attempting the playing of scales when
learning an instrument as a child. The first scales to be learnt were most
likely to have been of the Authentic Major type. This is still so for
instrumental beginners today.

The Authentic Major scale:

d–r–m–f–s–l–t–d' for example:

(doh = C)

doh

The concept of the Authentic Major should be easily understood. It is the
most commonly acknowledged scale in Western art and popular music.

Suggested songs

10   Go dung a Manuel Road
22   Oh me dad was a fisherman bold
29   Right tru, right tru, de rocky road

Music activities

KEY ▶

60 a Many song melodies use the notes of the Authentic Major scale. For
example, from Key Stage 2B Song collection, see those listed above.

60 b In imitation of the teacher, the children should first sing to solfa the
Authentic Major scale on C, ascending and descending
(**d–r–m–f–s–l–t–d'–t–l–s–f–m–r–d**), with the support of handsigns; then to
fixed pitch names – C D E F G A B C etc. Now ask the children to perform
the scale in similar ways, but to selected rhythms. For example:

Explain to the children that like the Natural Minor scale, the Authentic
Major is 'diatonic', i.e. it contains both tones and semitones (**m–f** and **t–d'**).

☆ Pupil's Book 4,
pages 40 and 41

60 c Page 41 of Pupil's Book 4 asks the pupil to change the fourth phrase to
provide a different sequence to follow the third phrase; for example:

Skill/Concept

61 · Working with the Authentic Major

Music activities

KEY ▶
☆ Pupil's Book 4,
   pages 42 and 43

61 a 'Tingalayo' is a calypso melody from the West Indies, where the donkey is a much valued and respected working animal. The song is written using the Authentic Major with doh = C.

The children might invent further verses for 'Tingalayo'; for example:

Me donkey read
Me donkey write
Me donkey snores in his bed at night.

or

Me donkey jump
Me donkey run
Me donkey he has a lot of fun.

61 b ☆ Reading Sheet 21

This has a two-part version of 'Tingalayo'.

KEY ▶

61 c The convention for key signatures in the major dictates that the F sharp in the key of G major is placed on the top line of the staff (treble clef). The key of D major requires that F sharp is placed on the top line and C sharp in the third space up of the staff (treble clef). In the key of F major the flat is placed on the middle line (treble clef).

EXTENSION ▶

61 d Children might care to find melodies in other sources of music which are Authentic Major and compile a list of the titles and the countries of origin, together with written analysis of the phrase structures and rhythm sets. For example:

Title	Country
Shepherds shake off your drowsy sleep	France – a carol from Besançon
Phrases	**Rhythm set**
A B C D C E – each two bars long	♩. / ♪ ♪ ♪ / ♩ ♪

You might index your findings on a suitable computer database program.

61 e ☆ Choral file 15: 'Early one morning'

The top part has a series of ascending–descending notes within each phrase. The final phrase, in particular, needs a positive but unforced vocal approach if it is not to sound tonally thin, strained and out of tune. The children should be encouraged to support the singing of the phrase with plenty of air, relaxed shoulders and neck, open vowels, a disregard for the consonants and a pitching focus about the level of the eyes.

Skill/Concept

62   Project: musical clocks

Music activities

KEY ▶
☆ Pupil's Book 4,
   page 44

 a   The children may care to research information about mechanical musical clocks, boxes, organs, pianos and various automaton. Examples might be available locally (cathedral, museum, collectors), and the children may have clocks that chime and musical boxes at home.

Skill/Concept

63 The Plagal Major (1)

▷ The Plagal Major scale encompasses the octave between s, and s – i.e. ascending – **s,–l,–t,–d–r–m–f–s**. Melodies using the Plagal Major have doh as the final note or key note. Such melodies are 'major' in tonality. The 'plagal' arrangement of the major scale notes (**s,–l,–t–d–r–m–f–s**) is different from that of the 'authentic' (**d–r–m–f–s–l–t–d'**).

Suggested songs

4 Cadet Rouselle (French)
5 Caragan, caragan (Scottish)
7 Di didl lan dan (Welsh)
14 Infant holy (Polish)
25 Old apple tree we'll wassail thee (English)
32 Trarira, der Sommer, der ist da! (German)

Music activities

KEY ▶

63 a European song melodies of the major scale variety are very often plagal in structure. Those included in the **Key Stage 2B** Song collection are listed above.

☆ **Pupil's Book 4, page 45**

Explain to the children that, like the Natural Minor scale, the Authentic Major is 'diatonic', i.e. it contains both tones and semitones (m–f and t–d').

Skill/Concept

 Puppet project

Music activities

KEY ▶
☆ Pupil's Book 4,
pages 46 and 47
and Reading
Sheet 22

 a The melody on page 46 of Pupil's Book 4 is based upon the Plagal Major and is a puppet song (words by Ned Washington; music by Leigh Harline). Reading Sheet 22 is also a puppet song. The children may care to develop a puppet show as a project involving several aspects of the curriculum, e.g. art, design and technology, history (the story), science (lighting). Although the given songs are about string puppets, the projects might choose to make rod-puppets for shadow puppetry – a traditional art-form in the East (Javanese Wayang puppets).

For a shadow puppet show it will be necessary to make a screen using a rigid frame (a large picture frame possibly), over which can be stretched semi-opaque material on which to cast a shadow. Scenery can be attached to the material. A concentrated light source will be necessary – a lamp of the angle-poise type is ideal.

The puppets can be simple cutouts, the shape being drawn on to card, and then cut out. The rods – knitting needles or thin dowel – are fixed by tabs of stiff paper of card to the back of the puppet. A jointed rod-puppet is achieved by the use of metal paper-fasteners or rivets and additional rods. Joints - knees, elbows, neck, waist – add considerably to the expressive potential of the puppet.

The story could derive from a myth or legend of a particular culture.

The use of angular melodic shape in the 'Pinocchio' and 'Puppet on a string' songs gives a musical dimension to the angularity of the string-puppet movements. Melodic shape is the way a series of notes are related to each other by interval – the pitch distance between succeeding pairs of notes.

EXTENSION ▶

 b ☆ Choral file 16: 'Bobby Shafto'

The Shafto family were a wealthy mine- and ship-owning family in Northumberland during the 17th to 19th centuries. Robert Shafto, who lived 1732–1797 had a notorious reputation for his unscrupulous treatment of women whom he seduced between business trips and then deserted. He was handsome, charming and a celebrated man of fashion who squandered his wife's fortune at the royal court in London. Bobby Shafto was MP for Durham from 1760–1779.

The melody should be sung with a light and unforced sound. The lower part has a number of rising jumps that will need a little care if the upper note is not to sound pinched and inaccurately focused. The vowels on the higher notes are open vowels and will encourage a wide and relaxed throat. The children should aurally anticipate the leap and focus the higher note at eye level.

Skill/Concept

| 65 | The Plagal Major (2) |

Music activities

KEY ▶
☆ Pupil's Book 4,
   page 48

| 65 | a

The Northumberland folksong ('Dance to your daddy') is written in the key of G major. The key signature of F sharp remains on the top line (as in the Authentic version of the Major) even though the pitch range is lower.

Drones are a common form of accompaniment to melodies, especially when they are played on melodic instruments such as the Northumbrian and Scottish bagpipes, the hurdy-gurdy (particularly popular in France at one time – 'Vielle à roue'), and the Indian sitar. Many of the dance melodies in **Key Stage 2** are enriched by adding a drone.

The drone is a single continuous note accompaniment, usually doh or soh in a major melody and lah or me in a minor melody. Occasionally, a two-note drone is used, e.g. doh with soh.

Voices can sustain a drone to accompany a song when the singers breathe at different moments.

EXTENSION ▶

| 65 | b

As an additional experience in distinguishing between the Natural Minor, Authentic Major and Plagal Major, ask the children to sing to solfa at a slow tempo the Authentic Major scale ascending and descending. Starting on the same pitch as the final note, they now sing the Natural Minor scale making the necessary interval adjustments. Finally, with the same starting pitch they sing to solfa the Plagal Major scale:

start: **d–r–m–f–s–l–t–d'–t–l–s–f–m–r–d=l,**
then: **l,–t,–d–r–m–f–s–l–s–f–m–r–d–t,–l,=s,**
then: **s,–l,–t,–d–r–m–f–s–f–m–r–d–t,–l,–s,=d.**

Song collection – alphabetic index

Song collection – analytical index

No	Title	Origin	Time signature	Tone-set/scale	Rhythm-set	Other feature(s)
1	Ao onipa dasani	Ghana	$\frac{2}{4}$	Plagal Major	*(rhythm notation)*	*Da Capo al Fine*
2	As we were a-fishing	England	$\frac{6}{8}$	Authentic Major + t₁	*(rhythm notation)*	Sequence Angular melody
3	Brian Ó Linn	Ireland	$\frac{3}{4}$	l–s–m–r–d–l₁–s₁	*(rhythm notation)*	Phrase structure: A B Bv Av
4	Cadet Rousselle	France	$\frac{6}{8}$	Plagal Major	*(rhythm notation)*	Half-bar entry
5	Cagaran, cagaran	Scotland	$\frac{3}{4}$	Plagal Major	*(rhythm notation)*	Step movement of melody
6	Come all you bold Britons	England	$\frac{3}{4}$	Dorian mode + s₁	*(rhythm notation)*	Anacrusis
7	Di didl lan dan	Wales	$\frac{2}{4}$	Plagal Major	*(rhythm notation)*	Sequence Mouth-music
8	Four white horses	Virgin Islands	$\frac{4}{4}$	m–r–d–t₁–l₁–s₁	*(rhythm notation)*	Syncopation game
9	Give me oil in my lamp	Trinidad	$\frac{4}{4}$	doh pentachord + l₁	*(rhythm notation)*	*Da Capo al Fine* Anacrusis
10	Go dung a Manuel Road	Jamaica	$\frac{4}{4}$	Authentic Major	*(rhythm notation)*	Syncopation game
11	Good morning, Missa Potter	Jamaica	$\frac{4}{4}$	doh hexachord + s₁	*(rhythm notation)*	
12	Grandfather still you may see at party	Sweden	$\frac{2}{4}$	doh hexachord + t₁–s₁	*(rhythm notation)*	Sequence *Da Capo al Fine*
13	Hot potato, pass it on	England	$\frac{4}{4}$	doh hexachord + t₁	*(rhythm notation)*	Game Sequence

No	Title	Origin	Time signature	Tone-set/scale	Rhythm-set	Other feature(s)
14	Infant holy	Poland	3/4	Plagal Major	*(rhythm notation)*	Sequence; Phrase structure: AABC
15	I was passing by	Liberia	4/4	$f–m–r–d–t_1–l_1$	*(rhythm notation)*	Anacrusis
16	I've a grey horse	Wales	2/4	doh hexachord	*(rhythm notation)*	Sequence; Melodic structure: climax
17	J'ai du bon tabac	France	4/4	doh pentachord	*(rhythm notation)*	Half-bar entry
18	Me father kept a boarding house	England	6/8	lah pentatonic	*(rhythm notation)*	
19	My love, my pride	Scotland	3/4	$l–s–fi–m–r–d–l_1$	*(rhythm notation)*	
20	My old hammer	USA	4/4	$s–m–r–d–l_1–s_1$	*(rhythm notation)*	Tied notes
21	Now the holly she bears a berry	England	3/4	Authentic Major $+ t_1$	*(rhythm notation)*	Anacrusis
22	Oh me dad was a fisherman bold	England	4/4	Authentic Major	*(rhythm notation)*	Anacrusis
23	Oh the country farmer went to Montreal	Canada	2/4	$m–r–d–s_1$	*(rhythm notation)*	Angular melody
24	Oh, the praties they grow small	Ireland	4/4	$f–m–r–d–t_1–l_1–s_1$	*(rhythm notation)*	Step movement of melody; Half-bar entry
25	Old apple tree, we'll wassail thee	England	6/8	Plagal Major	*(rhythm notation)*	Tied notes; Phrase structure: AABA

No	Title	Origin	Time signature	Tone-set/scale	Rhythm-set	Other feature(s)
26	Past three o'clock	England	$\frac{3}{4}$	doh hexachord + l₁–s₁	(rhythm notation)	Melodic ornamentation *Da Capo al Fine*
27	Planting rice is never fun	Philippines	$\frac{2}{4}$	Authentic Major + r' + t₁	(rhythm notation)	Sequence Melodic range: 10th
28	Raghupati	India	$\frac{4}{4}$	ta–l–s–fi/ fa–m–r–d–t₁	(rhythm notation)	Phrase structure: A B A B CD CD
29	Right tru, right tru, de rocky road	Jamaica	$\frac{4}{4}$	Authentic Major	(rhythm notation)	Syncopation: (notation) Game
30	Rise, sun, awaken	Pawnee	$\frac{4}{4}$	l–r–d–l₁–s₁	(rhythm notation)	The whole note
31	Speed bonnie boat	Scotland	$\frac{6}{8}$	soh pentatonic	(rhythm notation)	Melodic structure: climax; sequence; *Da Capo al Fine*
32	Trarira, der Sommer, der ist da!	Germany	$\frac{2}{4}$	Plagal Major	(rhythm notation)	

117

Song collection

- The Song collection in this Teacher's Book consists of vocal melodies chosen primarily because they are considered to be particularly suitable for this age range of pupil. Additionally, however, they contain musical features which are not only of particular relevance at this stage of aural and vocal development, but which also provide alternative material to assist further progress and provide wider musical experience.

1

Traditional Ghanaian, collected by Amoafi Kwapong

The words are those of the Akan people of Ghana.

'ɔ' is pronounced 'o', as in 'top'.

It is a marching song requiring a suitable drum accompaniment.

2

Traditional (England)

As we were a fish - ing off Hais - bor - ough light,

shoot - ing and haul - ing and trawl - ing all night, it was

win - dy old wea - ther, stor - my old wea - ther.

When the wind blows we all pull to - ge - ther.

t – l – s – f – m – r – d – t₁

2 We sighted a herring the king of the sea,
Says 'Now, old skipper, you cannot catch me.'
    In this windy old weather, stormy old weather.
    When the wind blows we all pull together.

3 We sighted a mackerel with stripes on his back.
'Time now, old skipper, to shift your main tack.'
    In this . . . etc.

4 We sighted a conger as long as a mile.
'Wind's blowing easterly,' he said with a smile.
    In this . . . etc.

5 We sighted a plaice that had spots on his side.
Says 'Now, old skipper, these seas you won't ride.'
    In this . . . etc.

6 I think what these fishes are saying is right.
We'll haul in our nets and we'll make for the Light.
    In this . . . etc.

The lighthouse referred to in the song – the Haisborough Light – is situated
between Cromer and Great Yarmouth on the East coast of England.
Although pronounced 'Haisborough', the correct spelling is in fact
Happisburgh.

3

Traditional (Ireland)

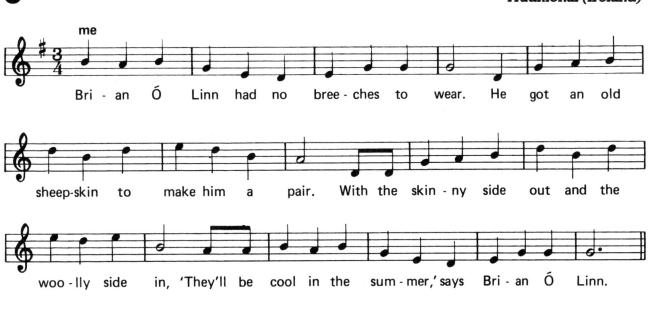

me

Bri - an Ó Linn had no bree - ches to wear. He got an old

sheep-skin to make him a pair. With the skin - ny side out and the

woo - lly side in, 'They'll be cool in the sum - mer,' says Bri - an Ó Linn.

l – s – m – r – d – l₁ – s₁

2 Brian Ó Linn had no hat to put on,
   So he got an old beaver to make him a one.
   There was none of the crown left and less of the brim,
   'Sure there's fine ventilation,' says Brian Ó Linn.

3 Brian Ó Linn to his house had no door.
   He'd the sky for a roof, and a bog for a floor.
   He'd a way to jump out, and a way to swim in,
   ''Tis a fine habitation,' says Brian Ó Linn.

4

France

soh

Ca - det Rous - selle a trois mai - sons, Ca - det Rous - selle a trois mai -

- sons, Qui n'ont ni pou - tres, ni che - vrons, Qui n'ont ni pou - tres, ni che -

- vrons. C'est pour lo - ger les hi - ron - del - les, Que di - rez - vous d'Ca - det Rous -

- sel - le? Ah! Ah! Ah oui vrai - ment! Ca -det Rous - selle est bon en - fant.

s – f – m – r – d – t₁– l₁– s₁

2 Cadet Rousselle a trois habits *(bis)*
Deux jaunes, l'autre en papier gris *(bis)*
Il met celui-là quand il grêle,
Ou quand il pleut, ou quand il grêle.
　　Ah! Ah! . . . etc.

3 Cadet Rousselle a trois gros chiens *(bis)*
L'un court au lièvr', l'autre au lapin *(bis)*
L'troisièm' s'enfuit quand on l'appelle,
C'est comm' le chien de Jean d'Nivelle.
　　Ah! Ah! . . . etc.

1 Captain Rousselle has houses three,
Three houses in the town has he;
They have no roofs, they have no floors,
They have no windows and no doors.
Up in the beams the bats are resting,
Under the rafters swallows nesting;
　　Heigh ho, say it in short
　　Captain Rousselle's a jolly good sort.

2 Captain Rousselle has horses three,
Three piebald, toothless mares has he;
They never whinny, never neigh,
They only sit and knit all day.
And since they don't like the stable,
They munch their oats at master's table.
　　Heigh ho . . . etc.

3 Captain Rousselle has greyhounds three,
Three lop-eared, bounding hounds has he;
Eating his soup, his meat, his bread,
Sharing his bedroom and his bed.
They have some rather funny habits,
They run away from bunny rabbits.
　　Heigh ho . . . etc.

The song is given with the original language version and an English
version freely translating the humour of the French.

5

Scotland

Cag - ar - an, cag - ar - an, cag - ar - an gaol - ach,
Hush - a - by, dar - ling, and hush - a - by dear, O,

Cag - ar - an, fogh - aint - each, fear de mo dhaoi - ne
Hush - a - by, dar - ling will yet be a he - ro;

Goid - idh e gobh - air dhomh, goid - idh e caoir - ich,
None will be big - ger, or brav - er, or strong - er:

Goid - idh e cap - ull 'us mart o na raoin tean.
Lull - a - by, lit - tle one, cry - ing no long - er.

s – f – m – r – d – t₁ – l₁ – s₁

2 Cagaran laghach thu, cagaran caomh thu,
Cagaran odhar, na cluinneam do chaoine;
Goididh e gobhair 'us goididh e caoirich,
Goididh e sithionn o fhireach an aonaich.

Lullaby, little one, bonnie wee baby,
He'll be a hero and fight for us maybe;
Cattle and horses and sheep will his prey be:
None will be bolder or braver than baby.

3 Dean an cadalan 's dùin do shùilean,
Dean an cadalan beag 'na mo sgùrdaich;
Rinn thu an cadalan 's dhùin do shùilean,
Rinn thu an cadalan, slàn gu'n dùisg thu!

Softly and silently eyelids are closing;
Dearest wee jewel, so gently he's dosing;
Softly he's resting by slumber o'ertaken;
Soundly he's sleeping and he'll waken.

A very old Scottish lullaby originally in the Gaelic language. The 2nd
verse in English suggests the period of history when Scottish clans
frequently raided their neighbours and enemies to steal the livestock.

6

England

Come all you bold Bri-tons where-'er you may be, I pray give at-ten-tion and lis-ten to me. There once was good times, but they're gone by com-plete, For a poor man lives now on eight shil-lings a week. *Der-ry down, down, down, der-ry down.*

l – s – fi – m – r – d – t₁– l₁– s₁

2 Such times in old England there never was seen,
As the present ones now, but much better have
 been.
A poor man's condemned and considered a thief,
And compelled to work hard on eight shillings a
 week.

3 Our venerable fathers remember the year,
When a man earned three shillings a day and
 his beer.
He then could live well, keep his family neat,
But now he must work for eight shillings a week.

4 The Nobs of Old England, of shameful renown,
Are striving to crush a poor man to the ground.
They'll beat down their wages and starve them
 complete,
And make them work hard for eight shillings a
 week.

5 A poor man to labour, believe me it's so,
To maintain his family is willing to go
Either hedging or ditching, to plough or to
 reap,
But how does he live on eight shillings a week.

6 In the reign of old George, as you all
 understand,
Then there was contentment throughout the
 whole land.
Each poor man could live and get plenty to eat,
But now he must pine on eight shillings a week.

7 So now to conclude and finish my song,
May the times be much better before very
 long;
May every labourer be able to keep
His children and wife on twelve shillings a
 week.

During the 1820s and 1830s the modest wages of the agricultural workers in Britain declined, causing much suffering and hardship to families. An attempt by the farm labourers of Dorset to organise a union to press for higher wages resulted in a group of them being prosecuted and transported to Australia in 1834 – they were the Tolpuddle Martyrs. This song was sung during those times.

7

Wales

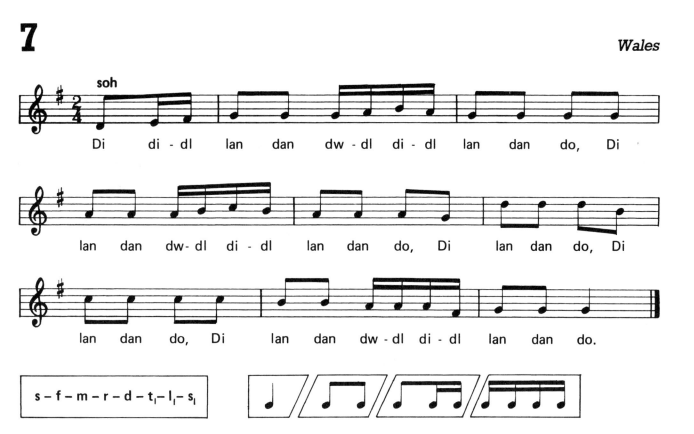

This wordless piece is reminiscent of Irish lilt music.

Pronunciation: 'di' pronounce 'dee'

'dwdl' pronounce 'doodle'

'do' pronounce 'doh'

8

Virgin Islands

Four white hor - ses on the ri - ver, Hey, hey, hey___ up to - mor - row. Up to mor - row is a rai - ny day. Come on and join our sha - dow play. Sha - dow play is a ripe ba - na - na, Up to-mor - row is a rai - ny day.

m – r – d – t₁– l₁– s₁

Activities

Clapping game

Two sets of partners form a square facing inwards:

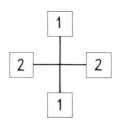

Beat 1: both couples slap their partner's hands – the 'ones' above shoulder level, the 'twos' below.
Beat 2: simultaneously, each person claps own hands.
Beat 3: as for beat 1, but 'ones' slap below and 'twos' slap above.
Beat 4: as for beat 2.
Beat 5: simultaneously, each person slaps one hand of both neighbours to right and left.
Beat 6: as for beat 2.
The sequence is repeated throughout the song.

9

Traditional (Trinidad)

Give me oil in my lamp, keep it burn-ing_____ give me

oil in my lamp I pray. Give me oil in my lamp, keep it

Fine

burn-ing_____ keep it burn-ing 'til the Judge-ment Day.

Once I had a he-ro fa-ther_____ Used to walk and talk with me Now he's

D.C. al Fine

gone on up to hea-ven_____ keep it burn-ing 'til the Judge-ment Day.

s – f – m – r – d – l,

10

Traditional (Jamaica)

This song is both a work song and a game.

Activities

Game

An even number of children take part. One is chosen to be the leader in the centre of a circle formed by the others. As the song is sung, the children in the circle walk round (section A). The leader sings and repeats section B for as long as he/she wishes, the circle providing the response. When the leader changes to section C, the children must quickly form pairs and continue walking in a circle. The person left without a partner leaves the game and the leader sings section D.

The song and game are repeated from section A with the leader singing 'Bruk dem two by two' at B and changing to 'Bruk dem three by three' at C. The game continues in a similar way.

A landlady's complaint to her lodger, Mister Potter. His daughter, Mary
Jane, with some help from the local pigeons, has been ruining the
landlady's kidney bean patch – and to top it all the rent has not been paid.

'piece a red peas' – kidney bean patch
'red Sally' – a variety of kidney bean

12

Traditional (Sweden)

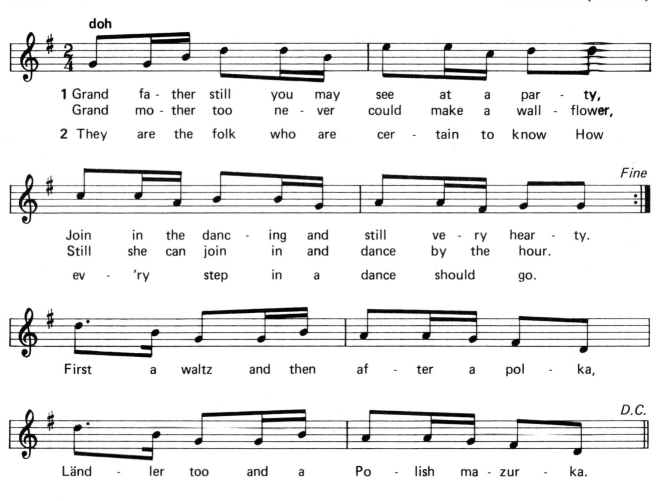

doh

1 Grand fa - ther still you may see at a par - ty,
Grand mo - ther too ne - ver could make a wall - flower,
2 They are the folk who are cer - tain to know How

Fine

Join in the danc - ing and still ve - ry hear - ty.
Still she can join in and dance by the hour.
ev - 'ry step in a dance should go.

First a waltz and then af - ter a pol - ka,

D.C.

Länd - ler too and a Po - lish ma - zur - ka.

l – s – f – m – r – d – t₁ – s₁

13

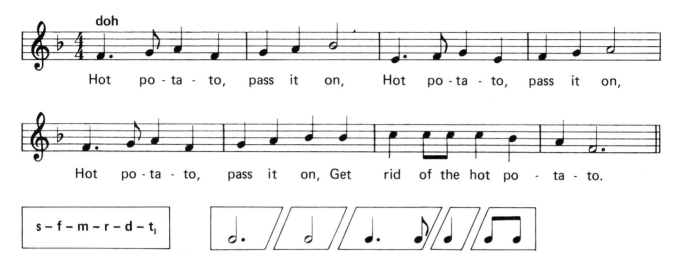

Hot po - ta - to, pass it on, Hot po - ta - to, pass it on,

Hot po - ta - to, pass it on, Get rid of the hot po - ta - to.

s – f – m – r – d – t₁

Activities

Game

The children sit in a circle; one child holds a ball. As the children start to sing, they pass the ball in one direction. The child holding the ball at the end of the song is 'out'. The game repeats until only one child is left. It is suggested that there are several circles consisting of, say, 8 children each.

14

Poland

soh

In - fant ho - ly, In - fant low - ly, For his bed a
Flocks were sleep - ing, Shep-herds keep - ing Vi - gil till the

cat - tle stall; Ox - en low - ing, Lit - tle know - ing
morn - ing new; Saw the glo - ry, Heard the sto - ry,

Christ the Babe is Lord of all. Swift are wing - ing
Tid - ings of a Gos - pel true. Thus re - joic - ing,

An - gels sing - ing, Now - ells ring - ing, Tid - ings bring - ing,
Free from sor - row, Prais - es voic - ing, Greet the mor - row,

Christ the Babe is Lord of all, Christ the Babe is Lord of all.
Christ the Babe was born for you! Christ the Babe was born for you!

s – f – m – r – d – t₁ – l₁ – s₁

15

Liberia

doh

1 I was pass - ing by, my bro -ther called me in, And he
2 sis - ter she

said to me, 'You bet - ter take time in life.' Peo - ple,

take time in life, Peo - ple, take time in life, Peo - ple,

take time in life, 'cause you got far way to go.

16

Traditional (Wales)

I've a grey horse you ought to watch him When he
runs no - one can catch him. Fal a roo - dle did - dle dal,
Fal a roo - dle did - dle dal. Fal a roo ho, ho!
Fal a roo ho, ho! Fal a roo - dle did - dle dal.

l – s – f – m – r – d

2 I've a fine saddle made of pigskin
   Bridle, reins and stirrups to ride in
   Fal a roodle diddle dal . . . etc.

3 I've a silk hat bought in Brecon
   Cost a pound at least, I reckon
   Fal a roodle diddle dal . . . etc.

4 I've a fine coat from a London tailor
   Fits me well and all been paid for
   Fal a roodle diddle dal . . . etc.

17

Traditional (France)

J'ai du bon ta - bac dans ma ta - ba - tiè - re, J'ai du bon ta -
I've some splen-did snuff in my jew- elled snuff - box, I've some splen-did

bac, tu n'en aur - as pas. J'en ai du fin et du bien râ -
snuff but there's none for you. On - ly the best in the shop I

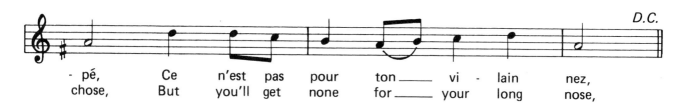

- pé, Ce n'est pas pour ton _____ vi - lain nez,
chose, But you'll get none for _____ your long nose,

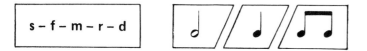

18

Traditional (England)

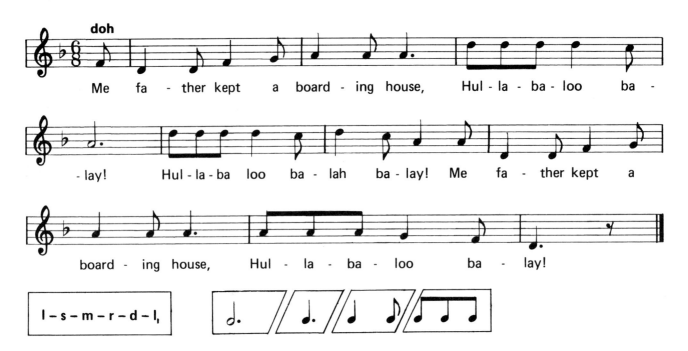

Me fa - ther kept a board - ing house, Hul - la - ba - loo ba -
- lay! Hul - la - ba loo ba - lah ba - lay! Me fa - ther kept a
board - ing house, Hul - la - ba - loo ba - lay!

l – s – m – r – d – l,

2 The boarding house was on the quay, (Hullabaloo balay!)
   But the lodgers were nearly all at sea, (Hullabaloo balay!)

3 A flash young fellow called Shallow Brown, (Hullabaloo balay!)
   He followed me mother all round the town, (Hullabaloo balay!)

19

Traditional (Scotland)

My love, my pride, my trea - sure, oh; My
won - der new, my plea - sure, oh; My son, my beau - ty
ev - er you; Un - wor - thy I to tend to you. Al -
- le - lu - i - a Al - le - lu - i - a.

s – f – m – r – d – t₁ – s₁

2 White sun and hope of light art thou!
Of love the heart and eye art thou.
Though but a tender babe I bore
In heavenly rapture unto thee.
Alleluia, Alleluia, Alleluia.

This lullaby, which originates from the Hebrides, refers to the Christ Child.

20

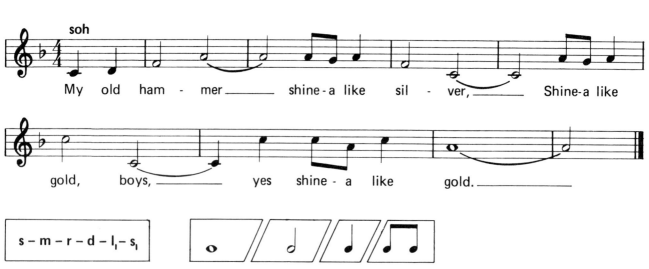

My old ham - mer _____ shine-a like sil - ver, _____ Shine-a like gold, boys, _____ yes shine - a like gold. _____

s – m – r – d – l, – s,

2   Ain't no hammer in-a this mountain,
    Shine-a like mine, boys, yes shine-a like mine.

3   I been working on-a this railroad,
    Four long years, boys, yes four long years.

One of the many songs that originated from the rail-building gangs of the
19th century. As a work song it should be sung at a tempo and with a vocal
style that reflects the laborious work of driving in spikes using a heavy
hammer.

21

England

2 Now the holly she bears a berry as green as the grass,
   And Mary she bore Jesus who died on the cross.
   (*Chorus*)

3 Now the holly she bears a berry as black as the coal,
   And Mary she bore Jesus who died for us all.
   (*Chorus*)

4 Now the holly she bears a berry as blood it is red,
   And Mary she bore Jesus who rose from the dead.
   (*Chorus*)

This carol originates from St Day, Cornwall, and always features in the
carol singing held in the square the week before Christmas.

22

Traditional (England)

1 Oh me dad was a fish - er - man bold And he
2 And ____ of - ten he'd say ____ to me You'd be

lived till he grew old, For he o - pens the pane and he
wise be - fore you go, Do you o - pen the pane and ____

pops out the flame Just to see how the wind do blow.
pop out the flame Just to see how the wind do blow.

If the flame don't flick - er 'e'd know That there's

not e - nough wind do blow, But if that sil - ly old

flame blow out Then there's too much wind to go.

d' – t – l – s – f – m – r – d

The mocking humour of this folksong belies the instinctive bravery of
Norfolk fishermen when faced with danger from the elements. See song 2.

3 When the north wind rough did blow
Then I lay right snug below;
But I opens the pane and I pop out the flame
Just to see how the wind do blow.
        If the flame . . . etc.

4 When the wind come out of the east
You'll be looking for snow and sleet;
But I opens the pane and I pop out the flame
Just to see how the wind do blow.
        If the flame . . . etc.

5 When the wind back into the west,
That'll come a rough in at best;
But I opens the pane and I pop out the flame
Just to see how the wind do blow.
        If the flame . . . etc.

6 When the south wind soft do blow
It's then I love to go;
And I opens the pane and I pop out the flame
Just to see how the wind do blow.
        If the flame . . . etc.

7 And my poor wife say to me
'We shall starve if you don't go';
So I opens the pane and I pop out the flame
Just to see how the wind do blow.
  If the flame . . . etc.

8 Now all you fishermen bold,
If you live till you grow old,
Do you open the pane and pop out the flame
Just to see how the wind do blow.
  If the flame . . . etc.

23

Traditional (Canada)

soh

1 Oh the coun - try farm - er went to Mon - tre - al, (Oh the)

- al. 2 Oh the wife of the coun-try farm - er went to Mon-tre - al, (Oh the) - al.

3 Oh the child of the wife of the coun - try farm - er went to Mon-tre- *(etc.)*

m – r – d – s₁

4 Oh the dog of the child of the wife . . . etc.

5 Oh the tail of the dog of the child . . . etc.

6 Oh the tip of the tail of the dog . . . etc.

The repeats of each verse could be sung by a second group of singers.

24

Traditional (Ireland)

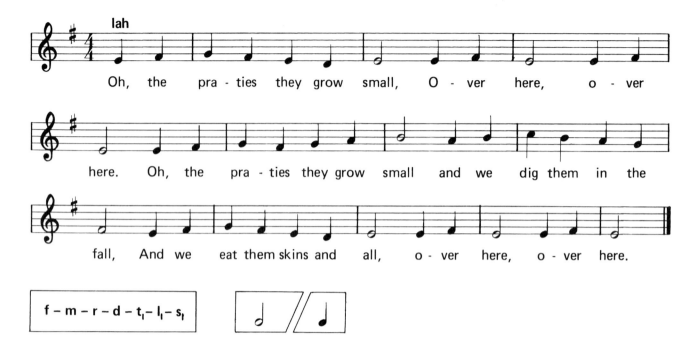

lah

Oh, the pra - ties they grow small, O - ver here, o - ver here. Oh, the pra - ties they grow small and we dig them in the fall, And we eat them skins and all, o - ver here, o - ver here.

f – m – r – d – t₁ – l₁ – s₁

2   Oh, I wish that we were geese,
    Night and morn, night and morn.
    Oh, I wish that we were geese
    For they fly and take their ease,
    And they live and die in peace, eating corn, eating corn.

3   Oh, we're trampled in the dust,
    Over here, over here.
    Oh, we're trampled in the dust
    But the Lord in whom we trust,
    Will give us crumbs for crust, over here, over here.

Between 1845–1849 Ireland suffered the 'Great Famine' caused by potato blight. The potato was the staple food of the country's poorer people. The famine resulted in a million deaths and forced another million to flee to America and Canada.

25

England

soh

Old ap - ple tree— we'll was - sail thee,— And hop - ing thou wilt bear; ___ The Lord does know__ where we shall be, To be mer - ry an - o - ther year. ___ To ___ blow well and to bear well, And so mer - ry let us be; ___ Let ev - ery man__ drink up his cup, ___ And health to the old ap - ple tree. ___

s – f – m – r – d – t₁ – l₁ – s₁

Spoken:
Apples now, hatfulls, capfulls, three-bushel
bagfulls, tallets ole fulls, barn's floor fulls, little
heap under the stairs.

Shout and stamp:
Hip, hip, hip, hooray!
Hip, hip, hip, hooray!
Hip, hip, hip, hooray!

In January it is the custom in parts of Somerset and Devon to 'wassail'
the cider apple orchards. The rituals, intended to drive away evil spirits and
encourage a good apple harvest, vary, but may include shouting, throwing
cider over a tree, and firing shotguns into the air.

26

Traditional (England)

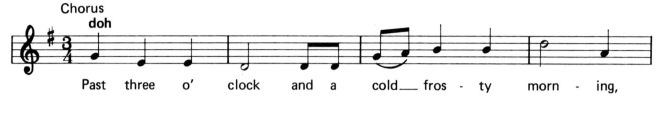

Chorus
doh

Past three o' clock and a cold fros-ty morn-ing,

Fine

Past three o' clock, Good mor-row mas-ters all.

Verse

Born is a ba-by, gen-tle as may-be,

D.C.

Son of the e-ter-nal Fa-ther su-per-nal.

l – s – f – m – r – d – t₁ – l₁ – s₁

2 Seraph choir singeth, angel bell ringeth,
   Hark how they rhyme it, time it and chime it.
       (*Chorus*)

3 Cheese from the dairy bring they for Mary,
   And, not for money, butter and honey.
       (*Chorus*)

4 Light out of star land leadeth from far land,
   Princes to meet him, worship and greet him.
       (*Chorus*)

27

Planting rice is never fun, Bent from morn till the set of sun. Cannot stand and cannot sit, Cannot rest for a little bit.

Planting rice is no fun! Bent from morn till set of sun; Cannot stand, cannot sit, Cannot rest a little bit.

r'– d – t – l – s – f – m – r – d – t₁

2 When the early sunbeams break,
You will wonder as you wake,
In what muddy neighbourhood
There is work and pleasant food.
(Chorus)

Rice is the staple food of the Philippines. Sowing and harvesting rice is
back-breaking work under a hot sun.

28

ray

Ra - ghu - pa - ti, Ra - gha - va Ra - ja Ram, _____
King - Ram of the Rha - gu ____ fa - mi - ly, _____

Pa - ti - t pa - va - n Si - ta - Ram: Si - ta - Ram jai - ya
You pu - ri - fy sin - ners Si - ta's ___ Ram. Hail to Si - ta, to

Si - ta - Ram, Pa - ti - t pa - va - n Si - ta - Ram.
Si - ta's Ram! You pu - ri - fy sin - ners, Si - ta's ___ Ram.

ta – l – s – fi/fa – m – r – d – t,

2 Ishware, Allah tere nam

Sabbe ko sanmati de Bhagavan
SitaRam jaiya SitaRam
Patit pavan SitaRam.

Some call you Ishware, some Allah,
O God give good thoughts to everyone.
Hail to Sita, to Sita's Ram,
You purify sinners, Sita's Ram.

This is a traditional Hindi prayer song to Rama, a re-incarnation of Vishnu, God of Love. Each section is first sung by the leader of the prayer meeting and then repeated by the congregation.

Mahatma Gandhi, who was instrumental in creating India's independence from Britain in 1947, used the song frequently at his daily prayer meetings. The second verse was written by Gandhi.

29

Traditional (Jamaica)

Right tru, right tru, de roc - ky road, Sing Char - ley Mar - ley call yu, Right tru, right tru de roc - ky road, Sing Char - ley Mar - ley call yu. A - ny gal me no like me no call to dem, Sing Char - ley Mar - ley call yu. A - ny bwoy me no like me no call to dem, Sing Char - ley Mar - ley call yu. Right tru, right tru de roc - ky road, Sing Char - ley Mar - ley call yu, Right tru, right tru de roc - ky road, Sing Char - ley Mar - ley call yu.

d¹ – t – l – s – f – m – r – d

Activities

Dance

The dance which accompanies this song requires the children to form couples and then to face each other in two lines. The couples join hands to form an arch, except the top couple who skip through the arch and rejoin hands again at the other end. As each pair in turn goes through the arch, the lines move up to fill the space that has been left.

The first couple now cast off and skip separately to the other end where they reform an arch. In a similar way each couple follows. The lines move up to accommodate the space that has been left.

30

Traditional (Pawnee [USA])

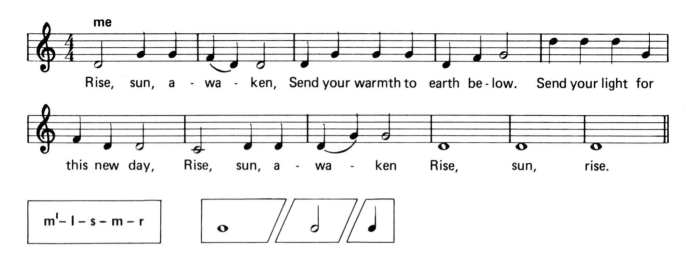

Rise, sun, a - wa - ken, Send your warmth to earth be - low. Send your light for

this new day, Rise, sun, a - wa - ken Rise, sun, rise.

m'– l – s – m – r

31

Traditional (Scotland)

soh

Speed, bon-nie boat, like a bird on the wing. On-ward the sai-lors cry:

Fine

Car-ry the lad that's born to be king O - ver the sea to Skye.

1 Loud the winds howl, loud the waves roar, Thun-der claps rend the air;

D.C.

Baf-fled our foes stand by the shore, Fol-low they will not dare.

s – m – r – d – l₁ – s₁

2 Though the waves leap, soft ye shall sleep, ocean's a royal bed;
   Rocked in the deep, Flora will keep watch by your weary head.

3 Many's the lad fought on that day, well the claymore could wield;
   When the night came, silently lay dead on Culloden's field.

4 Burned are our homes, exile and death scatter the loyal men;
   Yet ere the sword cool in the sheath Charlie will come again.

In 1745 Prince Charles Edward Stuart led a Scottish army in an attempt to
lay claim to the British throne. The brief but heroic campaign ended in a
nightmare of a bloody battle at Culloden and resulted in the persecution of
the clans by the Duke of Cumberland. 'Bonnie Prince Charlie' first fled to
the Isle of Skye before making his way back to France.

32

Germany

Tra - ri - ra, der Som - mer, der ist da! Wir
woll'n hin - aus in'n Gar - ten und woll'n des Som - mers war - ten!
Ja, ja, ja, der Som - mer, der ist da!

s – f – m – r – d – t₁– l₁– s₁

2 Trarira, der Sommer, der ist da!
Wir wollen hinter die Hecken
und woll'n den Sommer wecken.
Ja, ja, ja, der Sommer, der ist da!

3 Trarira, der Sommer, der ist da!
Der Winter ist zerronnen,
der Sommer hat begonnen.
Ja, ja, ja, der Sommer, der ist da!

1 Tra-la-la, the summertime is near
The garden calls to everyone
To go out there to greet the sun.
Cheer, cheer, cheer, the summertime is near!

2 Tra-la-la, the summertime is near
How good to see the hedgerows new
Play hide and seek, the summer's due,
Cheer, cheer, cheer, the summertime is near!

3 Tra-la-la, the summertime is here
The winter now has gone away
Look out to see a summer's day.
Cheer, cheer, cheer, the summertime is here!

This folksong is from the Rheinpfalz region and enthusiastically
celebrates the coming of summer.

Guidance for teachers

- This section sets out the underlying principles and aims of *Growing with Music: Key Stage 2B*. In addition, it contains useful information and explanation concerning the practical applications of the *Course programme*. Familiarity with *Guidance for teachers* is essential for the accurate interpretation and implementation of the principles, aims and contents of *Growing with Music: Key Stage 2B*.

Now read on.
This section is a must
for all you teachers.
It's essential reading,
take it from us.

The singing sound

- The guidance and exercises given under this heading in the Teacher's Book **Key Stage 2A** are still relevant to pupils. The suggestions given below will supplement the basic concepts of voice use and stimulate further development.

- It is important to recognise that a developing technique is only secured when it is integral to the singing of a song or choral piece. Exercises are a means of (i) focusing on a particular aspect of the singing instrument and (ii) raising the child's awareness of the potential of his/her voice. An increasing control over the singing voice gives the child the means and the power to communicate effectively a wide range of emotions.

Breathing

At the heart of successful singing is an understanding of the importance of breath control and the ability to utilise the breathing mechanism for the purpose of achieving phrasing, tone, intonation and dynamics.

Pupils at **Key Stage 2B** can be made aware of the diaphragm and the part it plays in breath control. The following exercises will help them to find the diaphragm and feel its movement.

Exercise 1
Ask the children to place their fingertips lightly at a point between the ribcage and just above the navel. The clothing should preferably be light. Now they should imitate the bark of a big dog in the form of several spoken 'woofs'. Did they notice that there was a violent movement inside the body under the fingertips? Did they notice that the flesh moved inwards as they barked and quickly returned as each bark was completed? Ask the children what was happening to the breathing as they barked and what followed each bark. The movement inside the body is that of the diaphragm, a muscle which aids the exhalation and inhalation of air from the lungs.

Exercise 2
The sudden exhalation of air experienced during the barking in Exercise 1 is similarly felt when blowing out candles on a birthday cake. Ask the children to imagine a tall, single candle flame which they are going to blow at gently in order to bend the flame without extinguishing it. The exercise could continue with each pupil blowing gently at the palm of one hand placed 15 cm in front of the mouth. Can they achieve a consistent

pressure of air on the palm for the duration of the breath? Are the children aware of the control they can exert by gently 'squeezing' the diaphragm? The exercise can be further extended by asking the pupils to sing 'noo' on the palm of the hand placed about 8 cm in front of the lips, first to a sustained single pitch and then to a short scale of notes.

Focusing the voice

If the voice is not to tire quickly, muscular tension is to be avoided, and a wide range of notes (tessitura) is to be achieved, then the singing voice requires to be focused at about eye level. This is slightly higher than that normally used when speaking. The following exercise will help to achieve this; it will also have the benefit of raising the soft pallet, widening the throat and cavities, and improving tone quality and intonation.

Exercise 3

ungh   ungh

Ask the children to sing the sound 'ungh', concentrating on the 'ng', to a sustained single pitch. Can they feel the roof of the mouth rise and a concentration on effort about the nasal cavities? Try a range of single notes.

As a further development try this:

Exercise 4

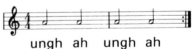

ungh ah   ungh ah

Encourage the pupils to retain the 'ungh' focus as they change to the vowel. The soft pallet should remain raised and the tongue move to a flat position. Again, experiment with a range of notes.

The following should be sung very legato and slowly:

Exercise 5

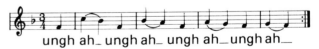

ungh ah_ ungh ah_ ungh ah_ungh ah_

The above should be attempted with a variety of vowels, including dipthongs, and at varying pitch levels.

Agility

With the support of a developed aural understanding, good breath control and a constant focus to the sound, children will be able to develop their vocal range and the ability to move from one pitch level to another with increasing ease and mobility. The *Growing with Music* song and choral repertoire will aid this development. At each Key Stage the songs demand an increasing vocal range and also an agility to move between notes sung in widely separated parts of the voice. For example, in **Key Stage 2B** Song collection:

'Oh the country farmer went to Montreal'
and in Choral file 16:

'Bobby Shafto'.

The following exercise will further this development. At first, sing quite slowly in order to achieve accuracy; then, in subsequent attempts, increase the tempo. Regularly change the pitch of the exercise.

Exercise 6

Consonants

Consonants give rhythmic definition to the words and are useful for accenting sung notes. Most consonants cannot be voiced so are interruptions in the singing sound. For these reasons, and the need to communicate a text to an audience, an ability to enunciate consonants clearly but quickly is an asset to any singer.

Here is an exercise which will demand precision and agility and raise the children's awareness.

Exercise 7

Over a period of time, the tempo of this exercise could be increased. Words incorporating other

consonants should be devised. Always sing with a relaxed jaw, tongue and lips. The singing tone should be light and the volume never more than moderately loud.

Dynamics

The importance of dynamics as part of the expressive dimension to singing is obvious. Children should always be encouraged to sing at varying levels of loudness. A constant demand for the children to sing loudly will give them a limited expressive capability and induce a raucous out-of-tune sound. An ability to control a great many gradations of volume will enrich the expressive armoury.

The following exercises encourage an awareness of crescendo (getting louder) and diminuendo (getting quieter). The ability to use the breath to support the change in volume is vital.

Exercise 8

Intonation

Singing in tune is part of any singer's craft. There are two major aspects to intonation. First, there is the need to sing in tune with oneself. Secondly, there is the need to sing in tune with others. In both cases, it is important for the individual to sing with accuracy and for true pitch relationships to be maintained throughout the piece. In the case of singing in parts, it is neccessary for all the singers to retain pitch consistency.

Intonation is dependent on several factors: breath control, focus, inner musical thinking and understanding, physiology, temperament and experience. The *Growing with Music* course programme and repertoire will help immensely, and working with solfa will prove invaluable.

The following two-part exercises will help to make children conscious of the need to listen carefully to each other. Children holding the sustained part will be very aware of the moving part. Both parts will discover whether they have remained in tune with each other when they arrive at the last note. Any

imperfection will be clearly heard! The exercises
should be sung firmly but quietly. Sing them to solfa
names, choose a slow tempo and vary the starting
pitch. Ask the children to sing firmly, but quietly,
and to listen carefully.

Exercise 9

Further and more developed exercises can be
found in Kodály's 'Let us sing correctly' (Boosey and
Hawkes).

Listening and appraising

Listening

Listening is at the heart of music making. Musical thinking is largely concerned with listening. When performing or composing one needs to first hear internally the sound that is intended. On hearing the sound the mind acts on the sense impression and passes judgement about its accuracy and about whether, among other things, any aspect needs to be changed.

Often we listen to music as an audience. The music we hear may be unfamiliar, when everything is new territory – or it may be familiar, when we find ourselves able to anticipate what is going to take place. Whenever the music is the product of another mind and not our own, our response will be conditioned by a number of important factors:

- the acoustics of the environment and our distance from the source of the sound;
- our expectations and emotions;
- our aural skills, experience and knowledge.

Through their involvement in the *Growing with Music* programme children will be helped to listen and respond to live or recorded music. As the children steadily acquire musical skills, concepts and a vocabulary of musical terms, their experiences of performing and composing give them a base upon which to listen critically and with enjoyment. This enables them to write with understanding and to converse about music they hear.

The notes on 'Listening' in the **Key Stage 2A** Teacher's Book still apply at this stage; however, live and recorded music pieces can now be of greater length. There are several points in the Course programme where suggestions are made for supportive listening-in-audience, e.g. *Skill/Concept index 3, 4, 10, 24, 27, 29, 39, 44, 45, 48, 49, 54, 55*. The teacher will undoubtedly find other opportunities to use recorded music to support current work.

Visiting performers can be an invaluable resource for supporting the children's musical development. They might relate to work in class by:

- performing music in styles with which the children are themselves working in their own performing and composing;
- performing the children's compositions and giving guidance;
- performing music using tone-sets, scales, rhythms and structures with which the children are familiar.

Appraising

Appraising is the process of attentive listening, analysing, forming judgements, exchanging information and views with others, evaluating, learning, and storing new knowledge for future situations. The process of appraising should lead to the child becoming an improved listener, and one whose aesthetic responses are increasingly developed. The child's judgements should be based on the skill to analyse music aurally, supported by a knowledge of the structural and expressive elements of music.

There are several modes of appraisal:

- evaluating a performance with an assessment of the skills of technique, expression, style and communication;
- evaluating a composition with an assessment of the skills of craftsmanship, handling the medium used, and communication.

The seeds of appraisal can be sown at an early stage of musical development by encouraging the children:

- to listen with care (National Curriculum: *listening attentively*);
- to think about what they hear – analysing with musical thinking (National Curriculum: *internalising it (music) for subsequent recall*), e.g. the tempo is fast; the pitch is high;
- to question what they hear – musical thinking (National Curriculum: *to criticise and evaluate*), e.g. how does what they have just heard compare to what they were expecting?
- to make decisions and to express their thoughts through written work and discussion, and to use musical terminology where appropriate.

When listening, understanding and evaluating compositions and performances a few points are worth remembering:

(i) The appraisal should always be positive.

(ii) There should always be an atmosphere of appreciation for the intentions, skills, and opinions of others. In the case of a performance the most important initial reactions are those of the performers, and the composer, if present.

(iii) Opinion should be based upon observable facts and a considered judgement. Everyone should be encouraged to justify preferences by assembling musical facts and demonstrating knowledge.

Composing

Composing needs to be seen as a vital ingredient in the process of learning. It is concerned essentially with encouraging pupils to extend the framework within which their music thinking takes place. As they compose they become increasingly aware of the opportunities and the problems of creating a piece of music which is more than a series of short rhythmic or melodic phrases. Composing is possible without using written symbols – but most teachers find that it often helps the process of thinking and planning if the memory is released for more creative tasks by encouraging the pupil to write down their musical ideas.

It is important to make a distinction between improvising and composing. Improvising is an excellent way for pupils to experiment with musical ideas in an immediate and spontaneous way. Improvising must be 'first-draft' effort – it is spontaneous. On the other hand, composing may involve several drafts. Although good composing frequently needs to have a quality of spontaneity in performance, it is inevitably the outcome of much thought, experimentation and manipulation.

More able pupils often show great powers of memory and some may well demonstrate composing ability without needing to write anything down. This should be encouraged. However, most young people who are learning how to use their acquired music skills and concepts to create pieces of their own making would find it difficult to compose successfully an extended piece by relying on memory only; they would seek to use some form of notation.

It is an aim of this Programme that pupils develop the ability to operate musically in both the written and unwritten musical traditions – by performing, reading, writing, improvising and composing. Improvising is to the centre forward as composing is to the team manager: both are essential to the success of the game.

Working with instruments

Playing a musical instrument demands more than the physical manipulation of a pipe, a string or a valve. Many instruments require technical skill from the player if they are to sound well; and some instruments need more technique than others.

At this stage of the Programme – as the pupils are coming to terms with the structural and expressive qualities of music, and the concepts and skills required to understand – it is helpful if instruments are less technically demanding so that most pupil attention is given to the musical task rather than the means of performing it. This is not to say that the quality of the sound and performance is not important; indeed, there may be those pupils who receive tuition out of class who take the opportunity to make good use of their instrumental skills when working in class, to the benefit of all.

As the pupils work with instruments, they need to be able to take musical account of their actions while playing – to be in control, not only of the instrument, but also of the musical event taking place. For example, a pupil who is using an instrument to improvise a melody which changes tonality in its third phrase needs to be aware of the nature of the change, how to obtain it on that particular instrument and how to perform it with appropriate expressive quality. The instrument, in the same way as the voice, becomes the means by which the pupil demonstrates his/her musical thinking – expressing externally his/her internal processing.

Even when reading from a part, the process is not mechanistic. The pupil needs to be making use of the skills, concepts and understanding they have acquired so that they are making sense of the written music and performing it accordingly. Audiences recognise musicians who perform with sensitivity, skill and understanding; usually, they do not appreciate the ingredients which make good performance possible.

Glossary

Definitions of musical terms additional to those found in the **Key Stage 2A** Teacher's Book.

Words relating to rhythm

Sixteenth note   Also known as the semi-quaver. Appears in notation as:

single – ♪

group of 4 – ♫♫

and in combination with eighth notes,

e.g. ♫ ♫ ♫ .

Tied notes   Two consecutive notes whose rhythm values are joined in notation by a tie.

For example: ♩‿♩

Delayed note   Results from increasing the rhythm value of the previous note by 50 per cent; shown in notation by the placing of a dot after the previous note. The delayed note is consequently of smaller value.

For example: ♩. ♪

Anacrusis   Note(s) at the start of a phrase which precede(s) the first strong beat of the phrase. In notation the value of the anacrusis note(s) is deducted from the total value of the last bar of the section/piece.

For example:

Half-bar entry   The start of a piece in quadruple metre two beats before the first full bar.

For example:

Syncopation   Rhythmic accents that do not coincide with the pulse.

For example:

Words relating to pitch

Relative pitch   The identification of pitch by means of recognising the constant pitch relationship between one note and another (e.g. doh-ray). If the pitch of doh changes, the pitch of ray moves also, to retain its position relative to doh. Relative pitch systems are most appropriate when using voice.

Fixed pitch   The identification of pitch by means of an absolute and unchanging standard (e.g. A, B, C etc.). Fixed pitch systems are most appropriate when using instruments.

Clef   The sign placed at the beginning of the staff to identify the position of a note of either fixed or relative pitch.

Treble clef (𝄞)   The fixed pitch sign placed at the beginning of the staff to identify the fixed pitch name G.

Tone and semitone   Measurements of pitch differences between two notes. The interval of a semitone (e.g. **m–f** is half that of a tone (e.g. **s–l**) and is normally the smallest interval used in music.

The sharp (♯)   Sign used in staff notation to indicate the adjustment of a note upwards by a semitone. The sharp can appear as part of a key signature and as an 'accidental' within any bar of music, i.e. an occasional sign.

The flat (♭)   Sign used in staff notation to indicate the adjustment of a note downwards by a semitone. The flat can appear as part of a key signature and as an 'accidental' within any bar of music, i.e. an occasional sign.

Tone-set   Written summary of the pitch of the notes used within a piece of music. The set is shown in solfa, arranged in either descending or ascending order of pitch.

Major   Word used to describe a tonality based on doh; also used to describe the diatonic scales on doh.

Minor   Word used to describe a tonality based on lah; also used to describe the diatonic scales on lah.

Natural Minor   The scale containing the notes l s f m r d t, l where the final is lah.

Key signature Normally the placing of a sharp or flat symbol on the staff immediately following a fixed pitch clef and indicating an adjustment needed (up or down a semitone) to the related note when it appears. The key signature may also appear 'blank', i.e. no sharp or flat symbol. Several flats or sharps can form part of the key signature.

Tonality When a phrase (or phrases) conform(s) to a tone-set of major (doh final) or minor (lah final) tonality.

Authentic Major The scale containing the notes d' t l s f m r d where the final is doh.

Plagal Major The scale containing the notes s f m r d t₁ l₁ s where the final is doh.

Scale Arrangement of notes written or performed in a descending and/or ascending order of pitch, usually containing tones and semitones (diatonic).

Passing note Unaccented note (*) linking by step between two accented notes.

For example:

Sequence Melodic fragment or phrase which is immediately repeated at a pitch higher or lower.

For example:

Words relating to structure

Canon Music with several or more parts each performing the same single melody. The parts enter independently and in imitation of each other at a point prior to the conclusion of the first structural phrase in the preceding part. Each part performs the music once only (unlike a round). A following part may imitate the preceding part using notes of the same pitch (unison) or 'transpose' the melody to another pitch.

Da Capo al Fine Form of wording used in written music which asks the performer to repeat a specified portion of previous material. The Italian words mean 'from the beginning until the word "fine" – the end'.

Melodic structure Construction of a melody by identifiable phrases which can be analysed and compared. The phrases can be identified as being the same, different or similar and labelled accordingly, e.g. A B Av – where the A phrase is different from B, but Av (varied) is similar to A.

Other words

Style Recurring rhythmic, pitch, structural and other features which identify examples of music as belonging to a particular composer, historical period, genre, tradition or geographical region of origin.

Copymasters

- These copymasters include Writing Sheet 1 and Writing Sheet 2 to provide a template for writing in rhythm-solfa and staff notation. The Worksheets are referenced in the Teacher's Book and should be distributed when needed. The Analysis Sheet can be used when the children are asked to analyse melodies; alternatively, they are useful for the teacher or pupil to complete in advance when setting a composing task. The Reading Sheets provide a variety of melodic and two-part material for reading practice. The Choral Files provide choral music in two and three parts. The Orchestral files provide a full score and parts for class instrument ensembles.

- Also included in the copymasters is a Teacher Lesson Planning Sheet and Record of Assessment Sheets for **Key Stage 2B**.

GROWING WITH MUSIC

Teacher Lesson Planning Sheet

Class:

Date(s):

Objective(s):

Skill/Concept reference	Development stage			Repertoire	Planned activities
	prep	mc	reinf		

What was achieved?

What happens next?

prep = prepare
mc   = make conscious
reinf = reinforce

Writing Sheet 1

GROWING WITH MUSIC

Writing Sheet 2

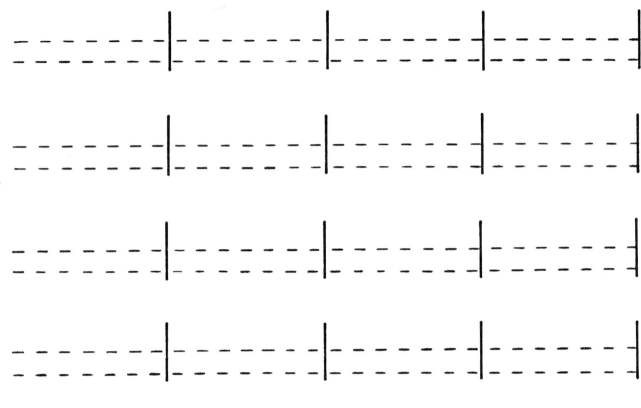

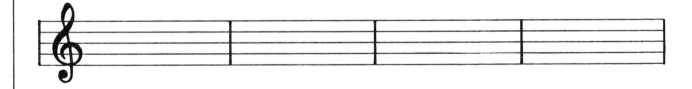

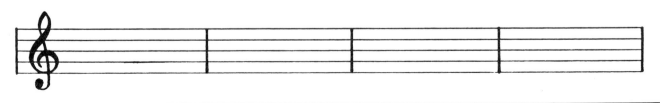

Worksheet 1

Compose your own song to these words and this structure, but in 𝄽 time.

- Use upper and lower sections of the pitch range.

- Include sequence, repetition and the anacrusis.

- Use Writing Sheet 2 if you wish to write in rhythm-solfa first.

(*Chorus*)
Well! Well! Well!

1 Some black chimney smuttings have blown this way,
So I need to wash it again today.

(*Chorus*)
It really is lucky, you see,
That this should now happen to me.

Other verses:

2 By turning so sour the milk can be
Some very good cheese for my grandchild's tea.

3 To make from soft thistledown I intend
A beautiful pin cushion for my friend.

4 Because I fell over upon the stair
My blue patchwork quilt I shall now repair.

5 The eggs are all broken about my feet
But warm scrambled eggs are a special treat.

6 My cottage which now has burned to the ground
Was subject to draughts and to leaks, I found.

The old woman's song on page 25 of *Pupil's Book 3* has these features:

Tone-set:	doh hexachord + l_1 + s_1
Pitch range:	section 1 – lower (m–r–d–l_1–s_1)
	section 2 – upper (s–f–m–r–d)
Sequence:	bars 7/8 and 9/10
Repetition:	bars 1/2 and 11/12

Worksheet 2

Group composing (or Musical consequences!)

Work with a partner. Follow your teacher's instructions.

Work in rhythm-solfa. Use the doh hexachord + l₁.
Use repetition and sequence. No anacrusis.

Phrase A

Phrase B

Phrase C

Now write out the complete melody in staff notation, with A A B C B C structure (doh = C).

GROWING WITH MUSIC

Worksheet 3

Composing a supporters' song

Remember that this is for a large crowd to sing. The first half of the song is rather like a hymn; the second half is more like a chant.

Write the rhythm of your song first.

2/4 | | | | | | | ‖

_____ _____ School is our name.   Play for   us   and play the   game.

| | | |

Now you're sure!   Now you know!   Come on!   Here we go!

| | | ‖

Make it good!   Make it flow!   Come on!   Here we go!

Now write your melody. Check the Analysis Box.
Notice that some words have more than one note.

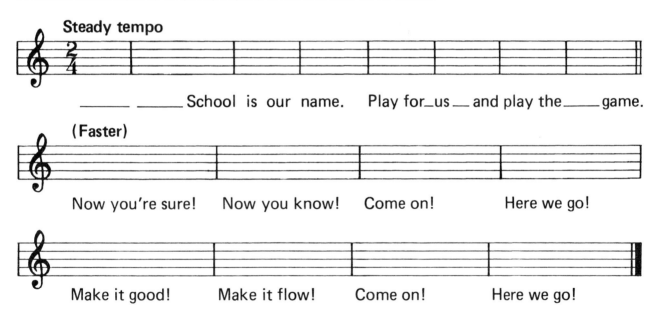

Steady tempo

_____ _____ School is our name.   Play for_us_ and play the_____game.

(Faster)

Now you're sure!   Now you know!   Come on!   Here we go!

Make it good!   Make it flow!   Come on!   Here we go!

This Analysis Box will guide you.

Number of bars	16
Phrase structure	A B C C
Notation to use	staff notation
Time signature	2/4
Rhythm-set	♩ ♫ ♩ z
Tone-set	lah pentachord + s + l
Special features	repetition/sequence

GROWING WITH MUSIC

Worksheet 4

Melody dominoes

In this game, each domino has one bar of melody.
By joining dominoes to each other, a melody is built,
bar by bar.
Each player sings the melody after adding a new domino.
Points are scored only if the melody is sung correctly.

Preparations

Making your dominoes

- The dominoes are prepared for you on Worksheets 6 and 7.

- Paste your copies of Worksheets 6 and 7 on to coloured card (a different colour from your partner), and then cut out your dominoes.

- Four of the dominoes have a treble clef, key signature and time signature; these are the Starter dominoes.

- The game should be played with the bar line on the right-hand side of the domino.

- There are 2 dominoes labelled 'Sequence', 2 labelled 'Improvise' and 4 labelled 'Repeat'.

- Worksheet 8 is a sheet for keeping score as you play the game.

- See Worksheet 5 for the rules of the 'Melody dominoes' game.

Worksheet 5

Rules of the game

1 Play as partners, with one set of dominoes. The aim is to make as high a score as possible. With practice, high scores can be earned by choosing to use dominoes which carry extra points (see top left corner of domino), and by choosing a high scoring **melody framework**.

2 First, partners agree the melody framework:
   (i) phrase structure;
   (ii) bars per phrase;
   (iii) change of tonality – these are shown at the top of your scoresheet (Worksheet 8).

3 The first player then places on the table, and sings to solfa, one of the four Starter dominoes (use only one per melody). Keeping the melody framework in mind, the second player places a suitable domino on the table to follow the first domino, and sings both bars to solfa.

4 The game proceeds in this way, with players in turn adding to the melody and singing the whole melody each time they add to it. Take care that the melody framework is correct because extra points will be earned from this at the end of the game. Use your partner's dominoes for repeated sections.

5 Each new domino correctly placed and sung earns 3 points; these are entered immediately on the scoresheet.

6 Extra points can be earned, as shown on the scoresheet – repeat bars, sequence domino, improvise domino and the extra points shown in the top left-hand corner of some dominoes.

7 When the melody is complete, the **melody framework** is checked and points totalled on the scoresheet accordingly. Play several times, trying to improve your score with each game played.

GROWING WITH MUSIC

Worksheet 6

Melody dominoes

GROWING WITH MUSIC

SMEP
SOMERSET MUSIC
EDUCATION PROGRAMME

Worksheet 7

Melody dominoes

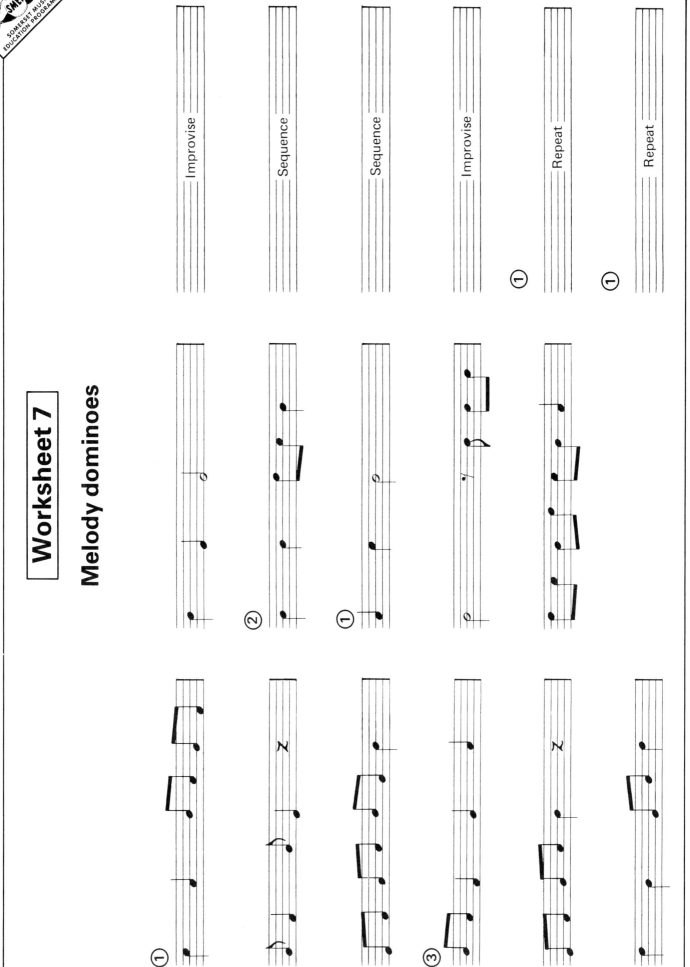

GROWING WITH MUSIC

Worksheet 8

Scoresheet

Melody framework

TOTALS

Phrase structure

A B A (Value 8 points) ☐ ☐

A B B A (Value 12 points) ☐ ☐ ☐ ☐

A B A C (Value 16 points) ☐ ☐ ☐ ☐

Change of tonality (Value 10 points) ☐ ☐ ☐

Bars per phrase

2 bars (Value 5 points) ☐ ☐

4 bars (Value 9 points) ☐ ☐

3 bars (Value 13 points) ☐ ☐ ☐

Points scored

Sing with new domino
(Value 3 points)

☐ ☐ ☐ ☐ ☐ ☐ ☐ ☐ ☐ ☐ ☐ ☐ ☐ ☐ ☐ ☐ ☐ ☐

Repeat a bar
(Value 2 points) (Twice per game only) ☐ ☐ ☐ ☐

Sequence domino
(Value 5 points) (Twice per game only) ☐ ☐ ☐ ☐

Improvise domino
(Value 7 points) (Once per game only) ☐ ☐ ☐

Domino extra points
(Value shown on domino)

☐ ☐ ☐ ☐ ☐ ☐ ☐ ☐ ☐ ☐ ☐ ☐ ☐ ☐ ☐ ☐ ☐

Sum total ☐ ☐ ☐

GROWING WITH MUSIC

Worksheet 9

Analysis sheet

Analysis

Number of bars ☐

Phrase structure ☐

Bars per phrase ☐

Staff notation ☐

Rhythm-solfa ☐

Time signature ☐

Rhythm-set ☐

Tone-set ☐

Other features ☐

☐

☐

☐

☐

☐

Options to consider

rests	canon
anacrusis	repetition
ostinato	sequence
dynamics	upper/lower sections of tone-set
tied notes	changing tonalities
passing notes	second part
delayed notes	voice/instruments
syncopation	purpose/style
chords	intervals

GROWING WITH MUSIC

Reading Sheet 1

Example A

Example B

American children's song

En-gine, en-gine, num-ber nine, Run-ning on Chi -

- ca-go line, If she's pol-ished how she'll shine,

En-gine, en-gine, num-ber nine.

Reading Sheet 2

Example A

Children's song

Rap - a, tap - a, rap - a too, Mis - ter Cob - bler mend my shoe.

Mend my shoe, and when it's done, I can walk and jump and run.

Example B

Children's song

'Oh', said the black - bird, sit - ting on a tree, 'I had a wife as

well as thee,

But she flew a - way and ne - ver came back, and

ev - er since then my head's been black.'

Reading Sheet 3

Example A

Children's song

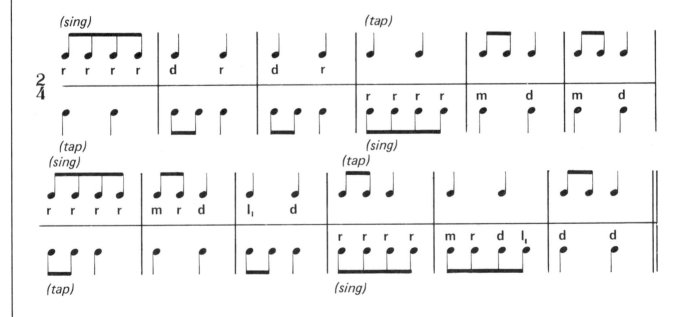

Example B

Reading Sheet 4

Example A

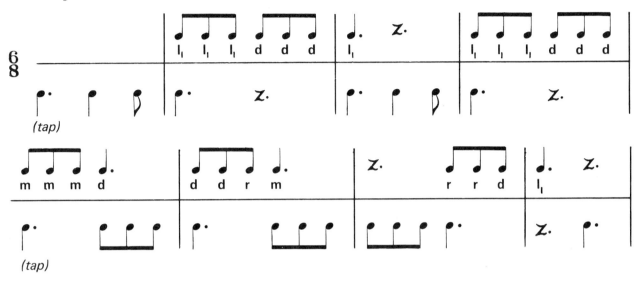

Example B

Z Kodály

Example C

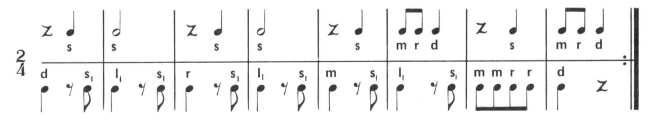

Reading Sheet 5

Example A

Bantu echo song

A-bi yo yo, A-bi yo yo, A-bi yo yo, A-bi yo yo,

A-bi yo yo, A-bi yo yo, A-bi yo yo, A-bi yo yo.___

Example B

Westminster chimes

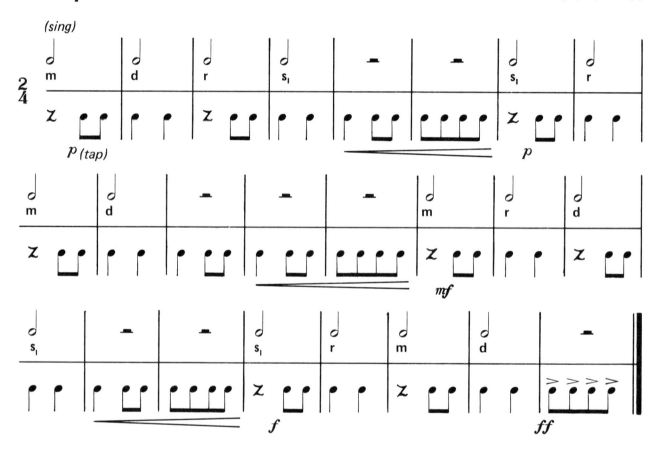

GROWING WITH MUSIC

Reading Sheet 6

Example A

Children's song

Example B

Welsh folksong

Example C

Children's song

Example D

Children's song

GROWING WITH MUSIC

Reading Sheet 7

Example A

French folksong

Example B

Flemish folksong

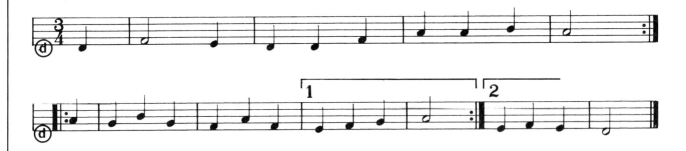

Example C

English folksong

GROWING WITH MUSIC

Reading Sheet 8

Example A

American folksong

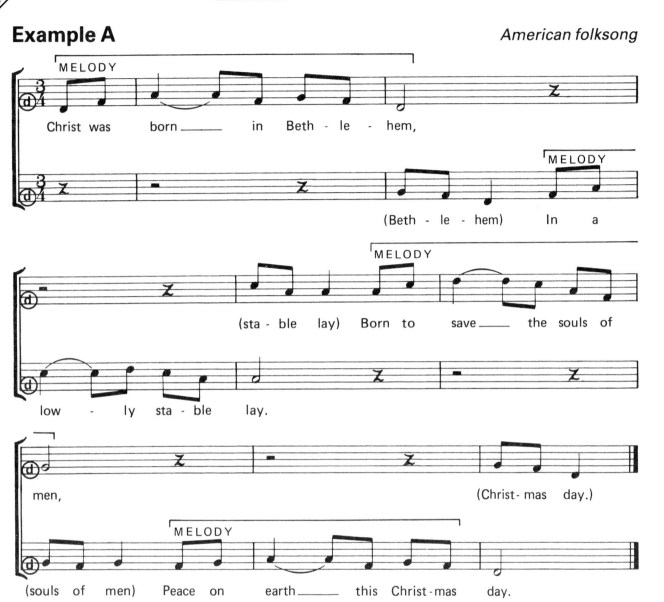

Example B

Reading Sheet 9

GROWING WITH MUSIC

Example A
English folksong

Jo - seph lay a - sleep - ing sound - ly when an an - gel did ap - pear.
Told him 'I am sent to warn you, Dan - ger threa - tens ve - ry near.

Bid the mo - ther quick - ly now her ba - by bring.

Save him from the an - ger of a jea - lous king.'

Example B
Children's song

Go and tell Aunt Nan - cy, Go and tell Aunt Nan - cy,

Go and tell Aunt Nan - cy her old grey goose is dead.

Example C
English folksong

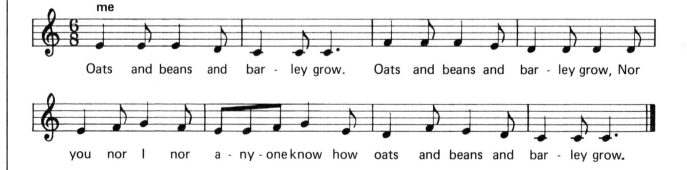

Oats and beans and bar - ley grow. Oats and beans and bar - ley grow, Nor

you nor I nor a - ny - one know how oats and beans and bar - ley grow.

GROWING WITH MUSIC

Reading Sheet 10

Example A
Children's song

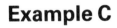

Example B
Children's song

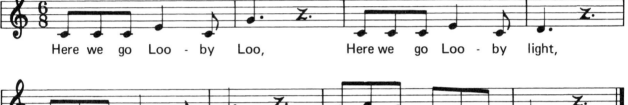

Here we go Loo - by Loo,   Here we go Loo - by light,

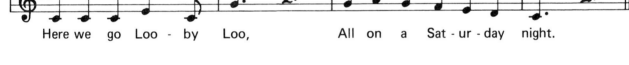

Here we go Loo - by Loo,   All on a Sat-ur-day night.

Example C
English carol

Jo - seph dear - est, Jo - seph mine, Help me rock our

lit - tle child. God will give you your re - ward in

heav'n a - bove: So prays the Mo - ther Ma - ry.

Reading Sheet 11

Children's song

doh

(On repeat)

John Smith, fel - low fine, Can you shoe this horse of mine?
Scam - per, scam - per well, Make the po - ny scam - per well.

Fine

Yes, sir, that I can, just as well as a - ny man.
Scam - per, scam - per well, Make the po - ny scam - per well.

D.C.

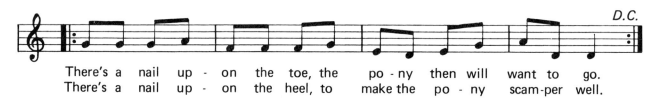

There's a nail up - on the toe, the po - ny then will want to go.
There's a nail up - on the heel, to make the po - ny scam - per well.

GROWING WITH MUSIC

Reading Sheet 12

English carol

GROWING WITH MUSIC

GROWING WITH MUSIC

Reading Sheet 13

Example A

Children's song

Example B

Children's song

GROWING WITH MUSIC

KEY STAGE 2B COPYMASTERS

Reading Sheet 14

Example A

Welsh folksong

ray

doh

Su - o - gân,   do not weep,   Su - o - gân,   go to sleep.

Su - o - gân,   have no fear,

Su - o - gân,   mo - ther's near.

Example B

lah   *

Example C

lah   *

© Longman Group UK Limited 1992

Reading Sheet 15

Example A

Example B

Dorset folksong

Come, I will sing to you. What will you sing to me?

I will sing you one oh! What may your one oh be?

One is one and all a - lone and ev - er - more shall be ___ so.

Reading Sheet 16

Example A

Israeli folksong

doh

He - cha - lutz le - man a' - vo - da, A' - vo - da le -
(Oh the young man works on the lands, makes the des - sert

- man he - cha - lutz. He - cha - lutz le - man a' - vo - da,
grow with his hands.) (Oh the young man works on the lands,

Chorus

A' - vo - da le - man he - cha - lutz. Zum ga - li, ga - li, ga - li,
makes the des - sert grow with his hands.)

zum ga - li, ga - li, Zum ga - li, ga - li, ga - li, zum ga - li, ga - li.

Example B   Da Pacem, Domine

Melchior Franck

GROWING WITH MUSIC

Reading Sheet 17

Example A

Example B

Reading Sheet 18

MELODY

Reading Sheet 19

Example A

Example B

GROWING WITH MUSIC

Reading Sheet 20

Hungarian canon

Reading Sheet 21

GROWING WITH MUSIC

Reading Sheet 22

soh

I _____ won-der if one day that you'll say that you

care, If you say you love me mad-ly, I'll glad-ly be

Fine

there, like a pup-pet on a string!_____

Love is just like a mer-ry go-round with all the fun of the fair_
I may win on the round-a-bout, Then I lose on the swings

____ One day I'm feel-ing down on the ground
____ In or out there is ne-ver a doubt

Then I'm up in the air. ____ Are you lead-ing me on?_
Just who's pul-ling the strings. ____ I'm all tied up in you!_

D.C. al Fine

____ To mor-row will you be gone? _____
____ But where's it lead-ing me to? _____

GROWING WITH MUSIC

Choral file 1

All night long

French folksong (arrangement: M Stocks)

With a steady tempo

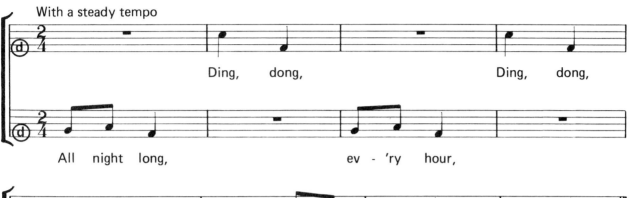

Ding, dong,   Ding, dong,

All   night   long,   ev - 'ry   hour,

Ding,   Dong,   ding, dong, Ding,   dong,   Ding,   dong.

Chime the bells from yon - der tow'r, a - ring - ing, a   ring - ing.

s – m – d
f – m – r – d

GROWING WITH MUSIC

Choral file 2

Warm days

(arrangement: M Stocks)

Slowly

Noo,   Noo,   Noo,   Noo, _____

Flow'rs in bloom   ev - ery - where,   soft per - fume,   Co - lours rare.

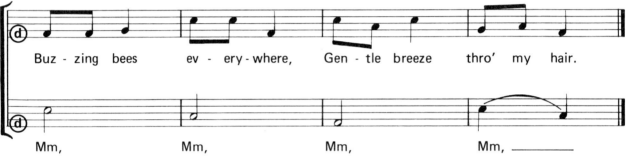

Buz - zing bees   ev - ery - where,   Gen - tle breeze   thro' my hair.

Mm,   Mm,   Mm,   Mm, _____

s – m – r – d
s – m – r – d

GROWING WITH MUSIC

Choral file 3

Who's that?

American children's song (arrangement : M Stocks)

GROWING WITH MUSIC

Choral file 4

Old house

Children's song (arrangement: M Stocks)

m – d – l₁
d – l₁ – s₁

Choral file 5

Sleep, baby, sleep

(arrangement: M Stocks)

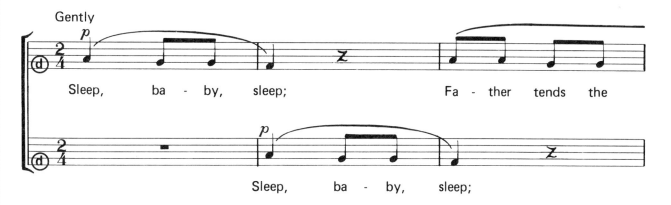

Sleep, ba - by, sleep; Fa - ther tends the

Sleep, ba - by, sleep;

sheep; Mo - ther shakes the dream - land tree and

Fa - ther tends the sheep; dreams come

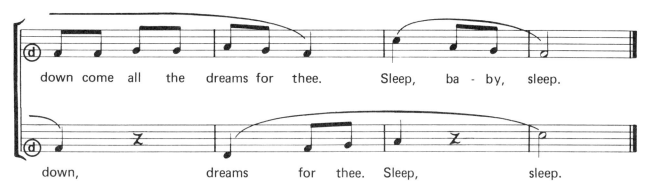

down come all the dreams for thee. Sleep, ba - by, sleep.

down, dreams for thee. Sleep, sleep.

s – m – r – d
m – r – d – l₁ – s₁

Choral file 6

Fire down below

English sea shanty (arrangement: M Stocks)

Choral file 7

Summer goodbye

German folksong (arrangement: M Stocks)

```
s – f – m – r – d
f – m – r – d – l₁ – s₁
```

GROWING WITH MUSIC

Choral file 8

Lavender's blue

Children's song (arrangement: M Stocks)

Andante

doh

mf La - ven - der's blue, dil - ly, dil - ly, La - ven - der's green,

doh

mf La - ven - der's pur - ple, La- ven - der's

When I am king, dil - ly, dil - ly, you shall be queen.

not just blue, La - ven - der's pur - ple.

l – s – f – m – r – d
l – s – f – m – r – d

GROWING WITH MUSIC

Choral file 9

Hush-a-bye, my little babe
Swedish folksong (arrangement: M Stocks)

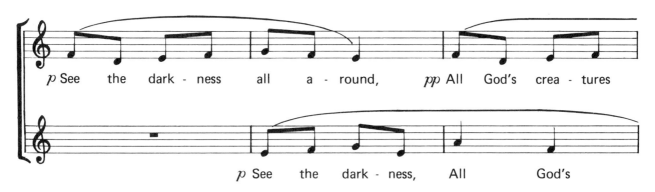

Choral file 10

Little Johnny dances

French folksong (arrangement: M Stocks)

Choral file 11

Coulter's Candy

Scottish folksong (arrangement: M Stocks)

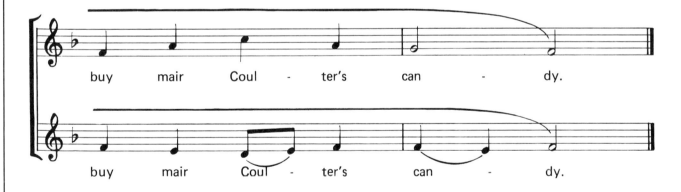

2 Mammy gie me ma thrifty doon, Here's auld Coulter comin' roon
Wi' a basket on his croon, Selling Coulter's Candy.

3 Little Annie's greetin' sae, Whit can puir wee Mammy dae
But gie them a penny atween them twae, Tae buy mair Coulter's Candy.

4 Poor wee Jeannie's affa thin, A rickle o' banes covered ower wi' skin,
Noo she's gettin' a double chin, Wi' sdookin' Coulter's Candy.

Choral file 12 (1)

Apple tree

Lajos Vass
Words by M Stocks

GROWING WITH MUSIC

Choral file 12 (2)

Apple tree (continued)

Un - a - ware of beau - ty. *f* Hark! Here

Pit - ter, pat - ter, pit - ter, pat - ter, *f* pit - ter, pat - ter,

comes the rain Not the time for chop - ping, so the wood-man

pit - ter, pat - ter, pit - ter, pat - ter, pit - ter, pat - ter, pit - ter, pat - ter,

goes a - way quick - ly, with-out stop - ping.

pit - ter, pat - ter, pit - ter, pat - ter, pit - ter, pat - ter, pit - ter, pat - ter,

mf In the ap - ple tree, ___

pit - ter, pat - ter.

GROWING WITH MUSIC

SMEP
SOMERSET MUSIC
EDUCATION PROGRAMME

Choral file 12 (3)

Apple tree (continued)

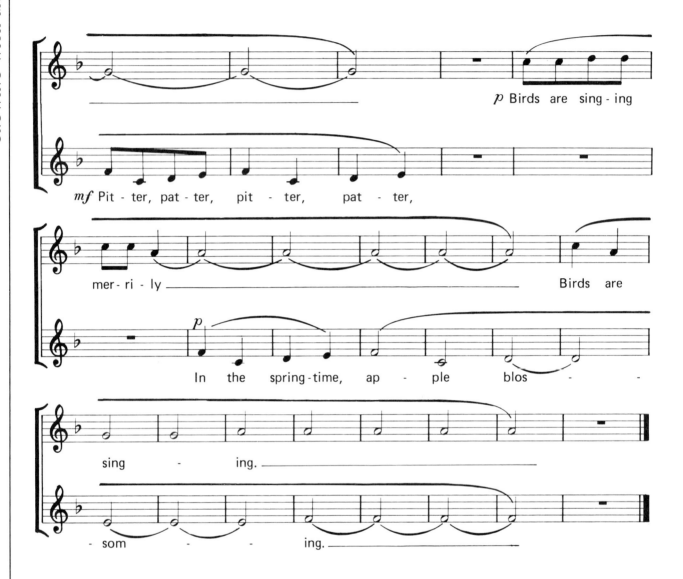

GROWING WITH MUSIC

Choral file 13 (1)

Coulter's Candy

Scottish folksong (arrangement: M Stocks)

Choral file 13 (2)

GROWING WITH MUSIC

Coulter's candy (continued)

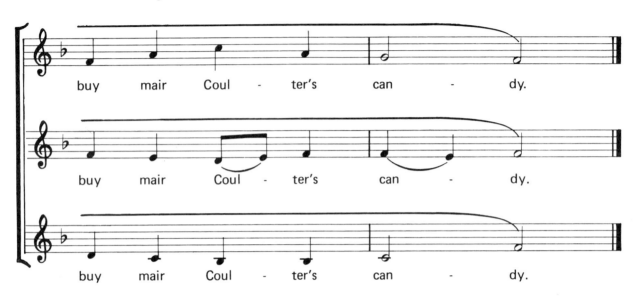

buy   mair   Coul - ter's   can - dy.

buy   mair   Coul - ter's   can - dy.

buy   mair   Coul - ter's   can - dy.

2 Mammy gie me ma thrifty doon, Here's auld Coulter comin' roon
Wi' a basket on his croon, Selling Coulter's Candy.

3 Little Annie's greetin' sae, Whit can puir wee Mammy dae
But gie them a penny atween them twae, Tae buy mair Coulter's Candy.

4 Poor wee Jeannie's affa thin, A rickle o' banes covered ower wi' skin,
Noo she's gettin' a double chin, Wi' sdookin' Coulter's Candy.

Choral file 14

Wraggle taggle gypsies

English folksong (arrangement: M Stocks)

GROWING WITH MUSIC

Choral file 15

Early one morning

English folksong (arrangement: M Stocks)

Early one morning, just as the sun was ris-ing, I

In the morn just at sun-rise,

heard a maid sing __ in the val-ley be-low.

I heard a mai-den in the val-ley be-low. __

'Oh don't de-ceive __ me! Oh, ne-ver leave __ me!

'Oh don't de-ceive or leave me!

How __ could you use __ a __ poor __ mai-den so?'

How could you use a mai-den so?'

GROWING WITH MUSIC

Choral file 16

Bobby Shafto

English folksong (arrangement: M Stocks)

GROWING WITH MUSIC

Orchestral file 1 | Score

The fox and the grapes

British folk dance (arrangement: M Stocks)

Orchestral file 1 | Part A

The fox and the grapes

At a good tempo

Orchestral file 1 | Part B

At a good tempo

KEY STAGE 2B COPYMASTERS

Orchestral file 2 | Score

The fisher laddie *(arrangement: M Stocks)*

Orchestral file 2 | Part A

Orchestral file 2 | Part B

© Longman Group UK Limited 1992

GROWING WITH MUSIC

Orchestral file 3 | Score (1)

This old man

(arrangement: M Stocks)

At a good tempo

Orchestral file 3 | Score (2)

This old man (continued)

Orchestral file 3 | Part A

This old man

At a good tempo

INTRODUCTION 4   MELODY

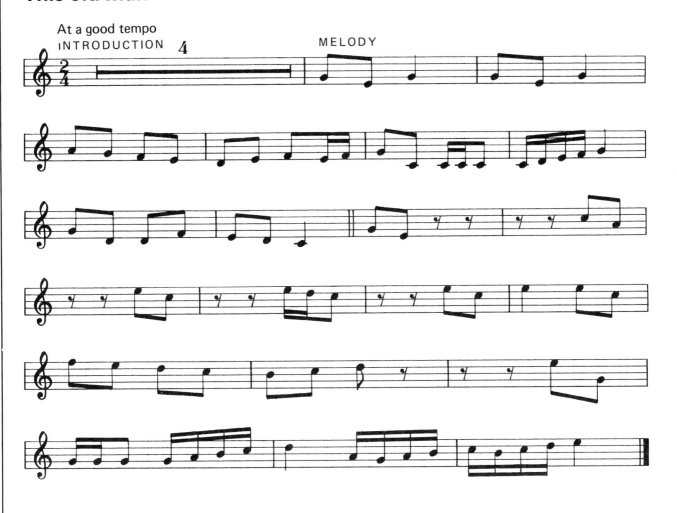

GROWING WITH MUSIC

SMEP SOMERSET MUSIC EDUCATION PROGRAMME

Orchestral file 3 | Part B

This old man

At a good tempo
INTRODUCTION

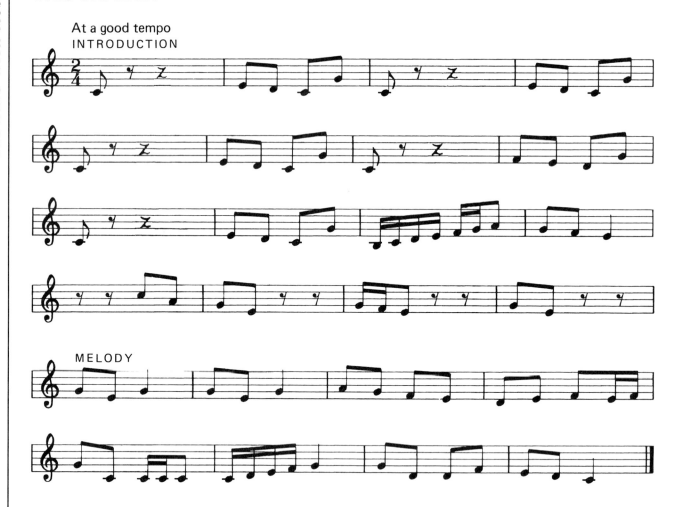

MELODY

(side) GROWING WITH MUSIC

Orchestral file 4 | Score (1)

J'ai du bon tabac

French folksong (arrangement: M Stocks)

Allegretto

© Longman Group UK Limited 1992

Orchestral file 4 | Score (2)

J'ai du bon tabac

GROWING WITH MUSIC

Orchestral file 4 | Part A

J'ai du bon tabac

Orchestral file 4 | Part B

Orchestral file 4 | Part C

Orchestral file 5 | Score

Oh Susannah — *American folksong (arrangement: M Stocks)*

Allegretto
Part A (MELODY)

Part B

Part C

Orchestral file 5 | Part A

Oh Susannah

Allegretto
MELODY

Orchestral file 5 | Part B

Allegretto

GROWING WITH MUSIC

Orchestral file 5 | Part C

Oh Susannah

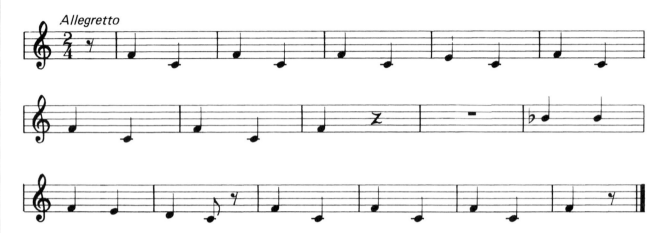

GROWING WITH MUSIC

Orchestral file 6 | Score (1)

I saw three ships

English carol (arrangement: M Stocks)

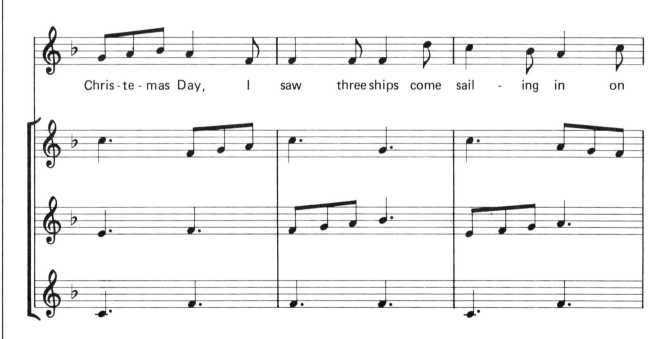

GROWING WITH MUSIC

Orchestral file 6 | Score (2)

I saw three ships

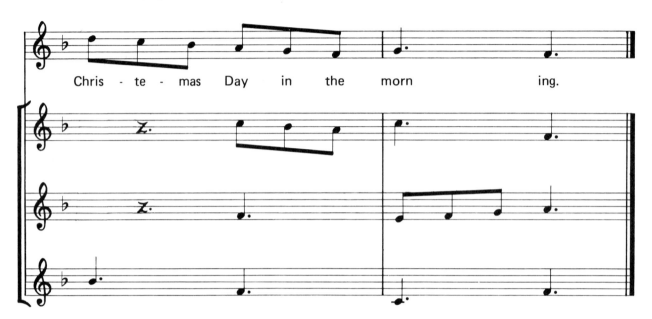

Orchestral file 6 | Parts A–C

I saw three ships

Part A

Part B

Part C

Orchestral file 7 | Score

Country dance

English folk dance (arrangement: M Stocks)

GROWING WITH MUSIC

Orchestral file 7 | Part A

Country dance

Orchestral file 7 | Part B

Orchestral file 8 | Score

Drops of brandy

English folksong (arrangement: M Stocks)

GROWING WITH MUSIC

Orchestral file 8 | Part A

Drops of brandy

Orchestral file 8 | Part B

Orchestral file 8 | Part C

GROWING WITH MUSIC

Orchestral file 9 | Score

Russian dance

(arrangement: M Stocks)

Orchestral file 9 | Part A

Russian dance

Orchestral file 9 | Part B

Orchestral file 9 | Part C

Russian dance

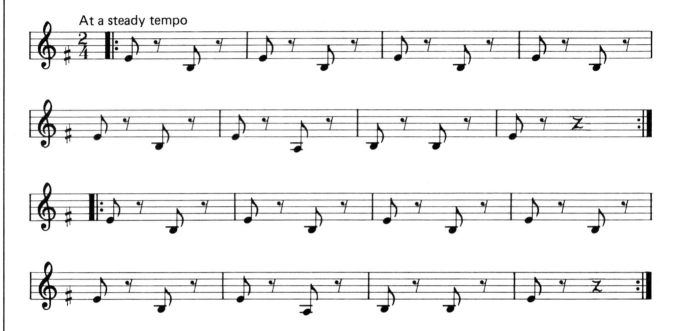

At a steady tempo

Orchestral file 10 | Score (1)

Shepherd's hey

(arrangement: M Stocks)

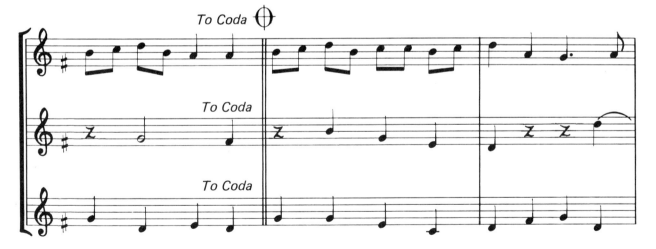

Orchestral file 10 | Score (2)

Shepherd's hey (2)

D.C. al Coda

D.C. al Coda

D.C. al Coda

rit.

rit.

rit.

Orchestral file 10 | Part A

Shepherd's hey

Orchestral file 10 | Part B

Shepherd's hey

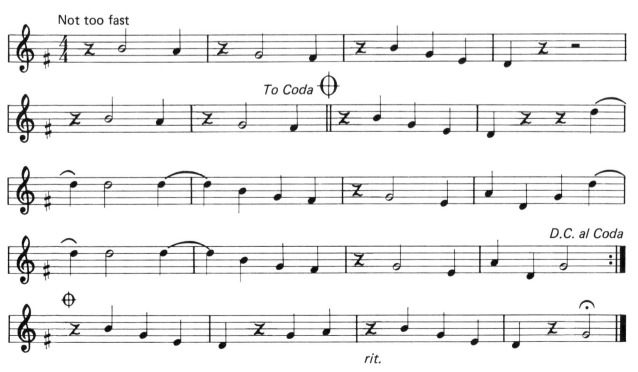

GROWING WITH MUSIC

Orchestral file 10 | Part C

Shepherd's hey

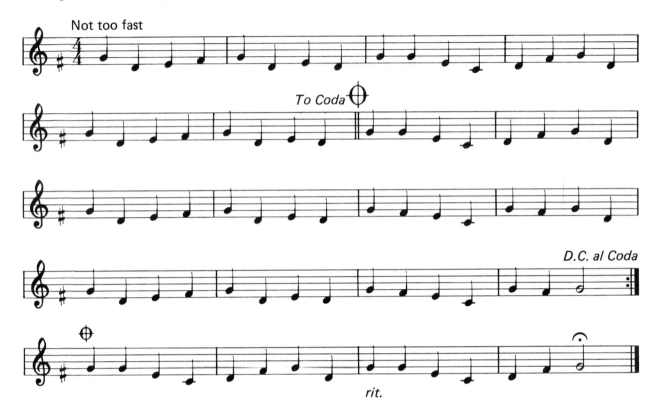

Orchestral file 11 | Score (1)

Rochdale coconut dance

(arrangement: M Stocks)

GROWING WITH MUSIC

Orchestral file 11 | Score (2)

Rochdale coconut dance

D.C. al Fine

Orchestral file 11 | Part A

Rochdale coconut dance

GROWING WITH MUSIC

Orchestral file 11 | Part B

Rochdale coconut dance

Orchestral file 11 | Part C

Orchestral file 12 | Score

Ukraine melody

(arrangement: M Stocks)

GROWING WITH MUSIC

Orchestral file 12 | Part A

Ukraine melody

Orchestral file 12 | Part B

Orchestral file 12 | Part C

Ukraine melody

The Ugsome Thing

A musical play for juniors to perform to infants

Cast:

Narrator 1	Villager 1	Girl
Narrator 2	Villager 2	Boy
The Ugsome Thing	Villager 3	Slaves
The old woman	Villager 4	Other villagers

Note to teachers

The music in this play relates directly to pages in Pupil's Book 3. The songs provided can be used, if preferred; but it is the intention that the pupil's own material be used as much as possible.

Here is a cross-reference from the songs in the play to the pages in Pupil's Book 3:
'The song of The Ugsome Thing' – page 14 (includes the 'Song of the Slaves')
'The old woman's song' – page 25
Dramatic music – page 40
'The building song' – page 48

The play

[The scene is a village, with a castle nearby. Enter NARRATOR 1 *and* NARRATOR 2.*]*

NARRATOR 1   There was once a monster called The Ugsome Thing.

[Enter THE UGSOME THING*]*

NARRATOR 2   He was round and fat and scaly and he had long teeth twisted like sticks of barley sugar.

THE UGSOME THING   *[with menace]* Heh, heh, heh, heh!

NARRATOR 1   He lived in a castle and had many slaves to work for him.

GROWING WITH MUSIC

SMEP
SOMERSET MUSIC
EDUCATION PROGRAMME

THE UGSOME THING   Heh, heh, heh, heh! They have to clean my castle and cook my food and till my fields and tend my flocks and herds.

['Song of The Ugsome Thing']

NARRATOR 2   Though they worked hard, he never paid them a penny in wages.

[Enter SLAVES*]*

['Song of The Ugsome Thing']

NARRATOR 2   The Ugsome Thing had a magic power, and if he could make anyone lose his temper, that person became his slave and had to work for him.

['Song of the Slaves']

NARRATOR 1   At this time, The Ugsome Thing had all the slaves he wanted, except for one.

THE UGSOME THING   I do not have a good washerwoman. My clothes are often dirty and badly ironed.

NARRATOR 2   One Monday, as he went through the village near his castle, he passed a cottage garden which was full of the whitest clothes he had ever seen.

[Enter OLD WOMAN, *hanging out her washing]*

   The clothes were like snow, blowing and billowing on the line stretched between two apple trees.

THE UGSOME THING   *[thoughtfully]* Mmmm.

NARRATOR 1   He decided to make the old woman who lived there come and do *his* washing.

THE UGSOME THING   It is very simple. I only have to make this old woman lose her temper and she will be in my power. Heh, heh, heh, heh!

NARRATOR 2   So the next Monday morning, when her clothes-line was full of the whitest wash possible, he cut the line with his knife.

THE UGSOME THING   *[cuts the line]* Heh, heh, heh, heh!

NARRATOR 1   The clothes tumbled on to the dirty grass. Surely that would make her lose her temper.

GROWING WITH MUSIC

NARRATOR 2   When the old woman saw what had happened, she came running out of the door, and instead of losing her temper she sang:

['Old woman's song' – verse 1]

NARRATOR 1   The Ugsome Thing was very angry and he gnashed his barley sugar teeth.

THE UGSOME THING   Grrrrrr!

NARRATOR 1   So the next day The Ugsome Thing visited the old woman again. He saw that she had milked her cow, Daisy, and that the milk stood in a pan in the dairy.

THE UGSOME THING   Heh, heh, heh, heh! I shall turn the whole pan of milk sour.

NARRATOR 1   When the old woman saw the pan of milk, she sang:

('Old woman's song' – verse 2]

NARRATOR 2   The Ugsome Thing was very angry and he gnashed his barley sugar teeth.

THE UGSOME THING   Grrrrrr!

NARRATOR 1   But he soon thought of another idea to make her lose her temper.

NARRATOR 2   On Wednesday, he turned all her hollyhocks in the garden into thistles, the red ones and the pink ones and the double yellow ones. She was very proud of her pretty garden.

THE UGSOME THING   Heh, heh, heh, heh!

NARRATOR 1   Surely that would make her lose her temper.

NARRATOR 2   But the old woman sang:

['Old woman's song' – verse 3]

NARRATOR 1   On Thursday, he did a very dangerous thing.

THE UGSOME THING   I shall stretch this piece of string across the stairs, so that the old woman will trip over it and fall. Surely that will make her lose her temper.

NARRATOR 2   The old woman did fall and hurt her knee, and had to hop on one leg to the shed to milk Daisy the cow. But still she sang:

GROWING WITH MUSIC

['Old woman's song' – verse 4]

NARRATOR 2   The Ugsome Thing was very angry and he gnashed his barley sugar teeth.

THE UGSOME THING   Grrrrrr!

NARRATOR 1   On Friday, The Ugsome Thing visited the old woman again. He saw her going to the hen house to collect the eggs. She had three white hens and they had each laid an egg.

NARRATOR 2   As she was walking past the apple tree . . .

THE UGSOME THING   Heh, heh, heh, heh!

NARRATOR 2   . . . he flipped a branch in her face and she dropped the bowl and broke the eggs.

NARRATOR 1   Surely, that would make her lose her temper.

['Old woman's song' – verse 5]

NARRATOR 2   The Ugsome Thing was very angry and he gnashed his barley sugar teeth.

THE UGSOME THING   Grrrrrr!

NARRATOR 2   But he soon thought of another idea to make her lose her temper. This was a very nasty one, because he was very, very angry indeed.

NARRATOR 1   On Saturday, The Ugsome Thing set on fire the old woman's cottage. Surely that would make her lose her temper.

NARRATOR 2   The flames shot up the walls and soon the thatched roof caught fire. It was the end of her cottage, and when The Ugsome Thing came along to see if the old woman had lost her temper, he found her busy baking potatoes in the hot ashes, and handing them round to the village children and singing:

['Old woman's song' – verse 6]

OLD WOMAN   *[to The Ugsome Thing]* Would you like to have a potato?

[Dramatic music begins]

GROWING WITH MUSIC

NARRATOR 1	It smelled so good that The Ugsome Thing took it and crammed it into his mouth whole, because he was very greedy, and some of it went down the wrong way.
THE UGSOME THING	Grrrrr . . . rrr . . . ughgh . . . ach . . . och . . .*[coughs]*
NARRATOR 1	He choked so hard with rage and hot potato that he burst like a balloon and there was nothing left but a piece of shrivelled, scaly, greenish skin.
THE UGSOME THING	A-a-a-a-a-a-a-a-ah! [*dramatic music ends*]
NARRATOR 2	A little boy threw it on the fire, thinking it was an old rag, and it burned with a spluttering yellow flame.
NARRATOR 1	By this time, most of the people in the village were lining up to have a baked potato, and while they waited they planned how they could help the old woman.
VILLAGER 1	We could build her a new cottage.
VILLAGER 2	She is always so kind to everyone.
VILLAGER 3	I could build the walls.
VILLAGER 4	I know how to make the roof.
VILLAGER 1	I've got some windows I could put in.
VILLAGER 2	And I could paper the walls to make it cosy and snug inside.

['The building song']

NARRATOR 2	By the time all the potatoes were cooked and eaten, her friends had promised the old woman all she needed for a new cottage.
NARRATOR 1	The new cottage was not old and tumbledown like the first one, but dry and comfortable with a sunny porch. The old woman lived there happily for many years with her cat, her dog and (of course) with Daisy the cow who had a new shed to live in.

This story is from *The Ten Tales of Shellover* by
Ruth Ainsworth, published by Young Puffin.

GROWING WITH MUSIC

RECORD OF ASSESSMENT: KEY STAGE 2 (FIRST ASSESSMENT)

NC: ENGLAND

SOMERSET MUSIC EDUCATION PROGRAMME

Class _____

Teacher _____

LISTENING AND APPRAISING

- Has recognised and identified same and different phrases in melody.
- Has discussed the structural and expressive elements of melody performed/listened to in class.
- Has used his/her musical memory to recognise and identify structural and expressive elements in music heard.

PERFORMING AND COMPOSING

- Has worked collaboratively with a partner to produce a written melody using rhythm-solfa.
- Has improvised melodic phrases as a contribution to a whole melody.
- Has worked with a partner on simple two-part rhythms.
- Has used the voice to support work in class and has used instruments to reinforce his/her experience.
- Has read/performed from rhythm-solfa notation.

Comments

Name

GROWING WITH MUSIC

SMEP
SOMERSET MUSIC
EDUCATION PROGRAMME

Class _____

Teacher _____

LISTENING AND APPRAISING

Has compared the structural elements of different melodies.

Has listened to and talked about music composed for specific occasions or events.

Has recognised the mood and character of known songs, and has identified the musical elements which contribute to this.

PERFORMING AND COMPOSING

Has shown an ability to compose a balanced melodic structure, using staff notation.

Has composed melodic pieces by comparing and contrasting phrases.

Has performed with others vocally and instrumentally from reading melodies.

Has connected internalised musical thinking with accurate vocal performance and has used a pitched instrument to perform known vocal melody.

Has read/performed from staff notation.

Comments

Name

GROWING WITH MUSIC

SOMERSET MUSIC EDUCATION PROGRAMME

Class _____   Teacher _____

LISTENING AND APPRAISING

- Has demonstrated a capacity for music thinking as a basis for amendment and improvement in his/her own composing and performing.
- Has described some of the essential characteristics of folk music.
- Has recognised and identified some of the expressive devices used in music to give a sense of climax.

PERFORMING AND COMPOSING

- Has composed a written melody for a specified occasion for performance by others.
- Has shown an ability to compose with extended structures.
- Has performed, with a partner, a rehearsed piece of music in two parts.
- Has developed good vocal quality and intonation and has used an instrument effectively within a musical task.
- Has performed melodically, in two parts, from staff notation and rhythm-solfa.

Comments

Name

GROWING WITH MUSIC

Class _____   Teacher _____

LISTENING AND APPRAISING

- Has described, discussed and undertaken simple analysis and evaluation of musical compositions and performances.
- Has understood the principal features of the history of music and has appreciated a variety of musical traditions.
- Has listened attentively to music of various kinds, recognising the main musical elements; had distinguished musical instruments, and has responded to changes in character and mood.

PERFORMING AND COMPOSING

- Has communicated musical ideas to others and has recorded compositions through the use of notations.
- Has devised and developed musical ideas within simple structures.
- Has performed in a group maintaining a simple part independently of another group.
- Has sung and played a range of music, controlling pitch, rhythm and dynamics.
- Has performed from notations interpreting signs, symbols and simple musical instructions.

Comments

Name

© Longman Group UK Limited 1992

GROWING WITH MUSIC

RECORD OF ASSESSMENT (LEVEL 2)

THE NORTHERN IRELAND CURRICULUM: MUSIC

Class _____

Teacher _____

RESPONDING TO MUSIC WITH UNDERSTANDING

Has initiated simple rhythmic patterns.

Has responded to familiar sounds within and beyond the classroom.

Has listened attentively to live and recorded music and has expressed his/her thoughts about it.

Comments

MAKING MUSIC

Has accompanied songs using tuned and untuned instruments.

Has sung a variety of songs as a member of a group.

Has invented symbols to represent sounds.

Has selected sounds in response to a stimulus.

Name

GROWING WITH MUSIC

Class _____   Teacher _____

RESPONDING TO MUSIC WITH UNDERSTANDING

- Has conveyed, through performance, the style and mood of the music.
- Has answered simple rhythmic patterns.
- Has listened attentively to live and recorded music and has commented on simple characteristics.
- Has discussed sound pictures and patterns composed by him/herself and others.

MAKING MUSIC

- Has played a tuned or untuned instrument as a member of a group.
- Has sung a variety of songs demonstrating some control of the voice.
- Has invented and interpreted symbols which represent particular sounds or patterns of sound.
- Has combined sounds in order to express mood and atmosphere.

Comments

Name

© Longman Group UK Limited 1992

GROWING WITH MUSIC

Class _____   Teacher _____

RESPONDING TO MUSIC WITH UNDERSTANDING

MAKING MUSIC

Has made appropriate suggestions about how music should be performed.

Has imitated and answered simple melodic patterns.

Has listened attentively to music and has recognised simple structural and expressive elements.

Has given reasons for his/her opinions about music s/he has heard.

Has performed individually on an instrument from memory or from notation.

Has sung a variety of songs, in unison and in parts, with control of phrasing, diction and tone quality.

Has interpreted patterns of sounds from graphic and traditional notation.

Has created short musical pieces which express mood and atmosphere.

Comments

Name

GROWING WITH MUSIC

Class _____   Teacher _____

MAKING MUSIC

RESPONDING TO MUSIC WITH UNDERSTANDING

Name	Has composed music using common structural and expressive techniques.	Has found ways of preserving compositions for later performances.	Has performed individually, by ear or from appropriate notation, music which demonstrates control in playing an instrument or in using the voice.	Has maintained an independent part on a tuned or untuned instrument as a member of a group.	Has used his/her listening skills to make judgements about music.	Has demonstrated an awareness of different musical styles.	Has created short improvisations from a given stimulus.	Has responded to musical features in the music s/he has performed or directed.	Comments

GROWING WITH MUSIC

SMEP
SOMERSET MUSIC
EDUCATION PROGRAMME

Class _____　　　Teacher _____

LEVEL B: ATTAINMENT TARGETS

Name	Has explored sound quality and has become familiar with the ways in which sounds are produced.	Has shown a greater ability to sing in tune with others; has fitted words to the melody where this is obvious; has controlled rhythm, speed and leaps in melody.	Has played simple melodic and rhythm parts, showing control over speed and volume, and has responded to simple signals of direction in performance.	Has created simple sound pictures, conveying an imaginative response to a stimulus and demonstrating an awareness of contrasts in music; has devised graphic symbols to represent the music.	Has worked co-operatively with others and has presented and performed music to the teacher and other audiences.	Had described the quality of sounds in terms of source, volume, distance and location; has discussed the characteristics of mood music; has recognised the sounds of instruments with a distinctive quality.	Comments

GROWING WITH MUSIC

SOMERSET MUSIC EDUCATION PROGRAMME

Class _____

Teacher _____

LEVEL C: FIRST ASSESSMENT

	Name	Comments
Has invented melodic phrases by comparing and contrasting phrases.		
Has connected internalised musical thinking with accurate vocal performance.		
Has used a pitched instrument to perform known vocal melody.		
Has recognised the mood and character of known songs, and has identified the musical elements which contribute to this.		
Has worked in partnership with others to improvise and invent melodic phrases.		
Has listened to and talked about music composed for specific occasions or events.		

GROWING WITH MUSIC

RECORD OF ASSESSMENT (LEVEL C)

CURRICULUM AND ASSESSMENT 5–14: SCOTLAND

Class _____

Teacher _____

SOMERSET MUSIC EDUCATION PROGRAMME

LEVEL C: ATTAINMENT TARGETS

Name	Has experimented with different combinations and qualities of sound to represent contrasting moods and effects.	Has sung confidently in unison, with some awareness of dynamics, phrasing and expression; has sustained a simple harmonic part.	Has displayed two-handed co-ordination in playing melodies and rhythms, sometimes using a form of written notation, paying attention to expression and contrasts.	Has created sound pictures which convey mood and atmosphere, displaying imagination and some awareness of structure; has devised a simplified form of notation to represent inventions visually.	Has worked co-operatively with others and has presented and performed music to the teacher and other audiences.	Has recognised the sounds of obvious groupings; has demonstrated aural retention; has given opinions of own music and that of others and has accepted and offered suggestions for improvement.	Comments

© Longman Group UK Limited 1992

GROWING WITH MUSIC

RECORD OF ASSESSMENT (LEVEL C)

CURRICULUM AND ASSESSMENT 5–14: SCOTLAND

Class _____

Teacher _____

SMEP
SOMERSET MUSIC
EDUCATION PROGRAMME

LEVEL D: ATTAINMENT TARGETS

Name	Has experimented and explored melodic, harmonic and rhythmic patterns and contrasts with a view to using them in inventions.	Has sung confidently, in unison and harmony, producing good vocal tone and clear pronunciation and demonstrating awareness of dynamics, phrasing and expression.	Has played confidently and expressively, sustaining more challenging melodies and rhythms on a range of instruments, sometimes using a form of written notation.	Has invented music with simple melodic, harmonic and rhythmic features and has shown imagination, awareness of structures and contrast; has represented inventions in simple notation.	Has worked co-operatively with others and has presented and performed music to the teacher and other audiences.	Has identified music in a variety of idioms; has discussed the effect of instruments on the character of the music; has demonstrated aural perception; has given constructive criticism.	Comments

© Longman Group UK Limited 1992

GROWING WITH MUSIC

SMEP SOMERSET MUSIC EDUCATION PROGRAMME

Class _____   Teacher _____

APPRAISING

Has discussed the structural and expressive elements of melody performed/listened to in class.

Has used his/her musical memory to recognise and identify structural and expressive elements in music heard.

COMPOSING

Has worked collaboratively with a partner to produce a written melody using rhythm-solfa.

Has improvised melodic phrases as a contribution to a whole melody.

PERFORMING

Has worked with a partner on simple two-part rhythms.

Has used the voice to support work in class and has used instruments to reinforce his/her experience.

Has read/performed from rhythm-solfa notation.

Comments

Name

GROWING WITH MUSIC

RECORD OF ASSESSMENT: KEY STAGE 2 (SECOND ASSESSMENT)

NC: WALE

SMEP SOMERSET MUSIC EDUCATION PROGRAMME

Class _____

Teacher _____

APPRAISING

Has listened to and talked about music composed for specific occasions or events and has described some of their musical characteristics.

Has recognised the mood and character of known songs, and has identified some musical elements which contribute to this.

COMPOSING

Has shown an ability to compose a balanced melodic structure, using staff notation.

Has composed melodic pieces by comparing and contrasting phrases.

PERFORMING

Has performed vocally and instrumentally from reading melodies.

Has connected internalised musical thinking with accurate vocal performance and has used a pitched instrument to perform known vocal melody.

Has read/performed from staff notation.

Comments

Name

NC: WALES

GROWING WITH MUSIC

SOMERSET MUSIC EDUCATION PROGRAMME

Class _____   Teacher _____

APPRAISING

- Has demonstrated a capacity for music thinking as a basis for improving his/her own composing and performing.
- Has recognised and identified some of the expressive devices used in music to create climax and repose.

COMPOSING

- Has composed a written melody for a specified occasion for performance by others.
- Has shown an ability to compose with extended structures.

PERFORMING

- Has performed, with a partner, a rehearsed piece of music in two parts.
- Has developed good vocal quality and intonation and has used an instrument effectively within a musical task.
- Has performed melodically, in two parts, from staff notation and rhythm-solfa.

Comments

Name

GROWING WITH MUSIC

RECORD OF ASSESSMENT: KEY STAGE 2 (END OF KEY STAGE STATEMENTS)

NC: WALE

SMEP
SOMERSET MUSIC
EDUCATION PROGRAMME

Class _____   Teacher _____

APPRAISING

Has discussed and evaluated a variety of music, including his/her own composition.

Has listened attentively to music and has made distinctions within its main elements.

COMPOSING

Has refined, completed and stored compositions.

Has devised and developed musical ideas within simple structures.

PERFORMING

Has performed in a group maintaining a simple part independently of another group.

Has sung and played a range of music, controlling pitch, rhythm and dynamics.

Has performed music from memory and has interpreted signs, symbols and cues.

Comments

Name

© Longman Group UK Limited 1992

Appendix

- The following pages show how 'Growing with Music' relates to (i) the criteria for assessment, and (ii) the Programmes of Study as expressed in the new music documentation for England, Northern Ireland, Scotland and Wales.

'Growing with Music' in relation to National Curriculum Programmes of Study (England)

KEY STAGE 2

PROGRAMME OF STUDY ITEM	'GROWING WITH MUSIC'
Pupils should:	**Observations and examples from the Programme:**
Memorise and internalise songs and musical ideas of increasing length and/or complexity.	The KS 2 Programme contains 155 songs in the Song collection, which are of increasing length and complexity.
Perform from simple notations and/or signals and understand a variety of musical instructions.	Based on performing and aural development, the pupils work with notations which enable extended musical thinking to take place, including staff notation and solfa pitch symbols/signs.
Sing an expanding repertoire of songs (unison and simple two-part), and pieces requiring a variety of vocal techniques, with increasing understanding and control of pitch, duration, dynamics, diction and phrasing.	The songs in KS 2 Song collection are carefully chosen to be appropriate to the age of the pupils and the complexity of the work being undertaken: *the Teacher's Book has guidance on vocal technique, with vocal exercises.*
Perform pieces/accompaniments on a widening range of more sophisticated instruments, with increasing dexterity and control of sound.	At KS 2B, instruments are used increasingly – partly to reinforce and support acquired concepts, and partly to provide experience of playing in small ensembles: *S/C 6, 16, 22, 14, 39, orchestral file.*
Maintain a part as a member of a group in a round or simple part song.	Graded choral material in two parts is included in KS 2B. This draws upon British, European and world music.
Play an individual instrumental part in a group piece.	Graded instrumental ensemble material is included in KS 2B, with the opportunity to work from scores and parts.
Rehearse and direct to develop skills and improve techniques.	An important feature of the Pupil's Books at KS 2 is that work with a partner or in groups is encouraged. This involves the constant use of techniques of negotiation and rehearsal.
Plan and present their own projects/performances, being aware of the need to communicate to different audiences.	The rich repertoire within the Programme provides an ideal basis for pupils to plan and present musical performances – most significantly because it is work prepared in class: *MUSIC IN OUR LIVES.*
Explore and use a widening range of sound sources.	This Programme uses vocal and instrumental sound sources. Other sound sources can readily be used as performing media, provided that they are appropriate to the work being undertaken.
Choose specific sounds and combinations of sounds to create a complete musical shape.	In KS 2B, there are many composing tasks in which pupils are asked to create melodic material of extended length which takes into account formal structure and changes of tonality.
Develop musical ideas through improvising, composing and arranging.	The Programme requires pupils to work with music and develop ideas particularly through improvising and composing.
Create music in response to a range of stimuli, using appropriate musical structures.	The Pupil's Books regularly ask pupils to respond to a range of stimuli, including verse, 'moods', specific occasions, drama, dance: *MUSIC IN OUR LIVES.* Composing is a strong feature throughout and there are opportunities to present performances.
Record and communicate musical ideas through notations which define the timbre, dynamics, duration, and, where appropriate, pitch.	Various forms of notation are used and suggestions are made to the pupils from time to time about the value of recording their work.

'Growing with Music' in relation to
National Curriculum Programmes of Study (England)

KEY
STAGE
2

PROGRAMME OF STUDY ITEM	'GROWING WITH MUSIC'
Pupils should:	**Observations and examples from the Programme:**
Develop their understanding of musical elements, and ability to describe them in appropriate vocabulary, and to interpret some of the signs related to them.	Pupils develop a working knowledge of musical elements, including relative and fixed pitch, simple and compound metres, rhythm, vocal and instrumental ensembles (texture) and form (structure).
Learn to distinguish sounds made by a range of instruments, individually and in combination.	A range of pitched and unpitched instruments are recommended for use in this Programme.
Listen to a range of instrumental and vocal music from early, classical and later periods.	The Programme includes musical examples from different periods in European history. The pupils work with many of the musical devices employed in these times.
Listen to the work of influential composers and learn something of their social and historical context and importance to the development of musical traditions.	The repertoire contains music from all the continents of the world, and the Teacher's Book frequently gives background information about the material and its origins, as well as guidance on listening to recorded music.
Talk about music heard in class, including their own compositions and performances.	Pupils analyse and evaluate music they encounter. This informs their performing and composing and includes syncopation, tonality and a progressively extended pitch-range.

(S/C = Skill/Comcept)

'Growing with Music' in relation to National Curriculum Programmes of Study (Northern Ireland)

KEY STAGE 2

PROGRAMME OF STUDY ITEM   'GROWING WITH MUSIC'

Pupils should have opportunities to:	Observations and examples from the Programme:
Recall and invent simple melodic patterns using voices, instruments or electronic media.	Based upon the large repertoire of vocal and instrumental melody in the Programme, pupils are constantly working with a rich range of memorised melodic material.
Recognise and distinguish between: duration, pace, dynamics, pitch, texture, timbre, structure, silence.	Pupils develop a working knowledge of musical elements, including relative and fixed pitch, simple and compound metres, rhythm, vocal and instrumental ensembles (texture) and form (structure).
Invent and play simple accompaniments, using a wide variety of sound sources.	In the Key Stage 2B Programme, instruments are used increasingly – partly to reinforce and support acquired concepts, and partly to provide experience of playing in small ensembles: *S/C 6, 16, 22, 14, 39, orchestral file.*
Create short musical pieces which draw upon their growing awareness of musical ideas and concepts.	The Programme requires pupils to work with music and develop ideas particularly through improvising and composing.
Represent patterns of sound by symbols.	Based on performing and aural development, the pupils work with notations which enable extended musical thinking to take place, including staff notation and solfa pitch symbols/signs.
Interpret patterns of sound, using graphic and standard notation as the need arises, in composition and performance.	Various forms of notation are used in the Programme and suggestions are made to the pupils from time to time about the value of recording their work.
Use information technology to extend their range of musical experiences.	This Programme uses vocal and instrumental sound sources. Other sound sources can readily be used as performing media, provided that they are appropriate to the work being undertaken.
Sing a variety of songs in unison and in parts.	The Key Stage 2 Programme contains 155 songs in the Song collection, which are of increasing length and complexity. Graded choral material in two parts is included in the Programme. This draws upon British, European and world music.
Perform songs and accompaniments with increased control, confidence and expression.	The songs in the Key Stage 2 Song collection are carefully chosen to be appropriate to the age of the pupils and the complexity of the work being undertaken: *the Teacher's Book has guidance on vocal technique, with vocal exercises.*
Organise and participate in group performances of their own and others' compositions using voices and tuned and untuned instruments.	The Pupil's Books regularly ask pupils to respond to a range of stimuli, including verse, 'moods', specific occasions, drama, dance: *MUSIC IN OUR LIVES.* Composing is a strong feature throughout the Programme and there are opportunities to present performances.
Increase control of pitch, rhythm and dynamics when composing and performing.	The Programme is built upon a sequence of basic music skills and concepts which ensure progression and an increase of control.
Play or sing an individual part in a group piece.	An important feature of the Pupil's Books at Key Stage 2 is that work with a partner or in groups is encouraged. This involves the constant use of techniques of negotiation and rehearsal.

(S/C = Skill/Concept)

'Growing with Music' in relation to National Curriculum Programmes of Study (Northern Ireland)

KEY
STAGE
2

PROGRAMME OF STUDY ITEM   'GROWING WITH MUSIC'

Pupils should have opportunities to:	Observations and examples from the Programme:
Suggest how music should be performed to take account of style and mood.	In the Key Stage 2B Programme, there are many composing tasks in which pupils are asked to create music of appropriate mood for given situations, and to understand why particular effects are obtained.
Become involved, if possible, in community musical activity.	The rich repertoire within the Programme provides an ideal basis for pupils to plan and present musical performances – most significantly because it is work prepared in class: *MUSIC IN OUR LIVES.*
Discuss and comment on musical detail, mood and characteristics of live and recorded music in different styles.	The Programme addresses musical styles, including typical structural and expressive features, all of which are ingredients of the Programme's progressive structure: *S/C 24, 35, 44, 54, 58, 62, 64.*
Recognise the sound of some common instruments and combinations of instruments.	Graded instrumental ensemble material is included in the Programme, with the opportunity to work from scores and parts.
Develop some awareness of the social, historical or cultural context of some of the music they hear and perform.	The repertoire contains music from all the continents of the world, and the Teacher's Book frequently gives background information about the material and its origins, as well as guidance on listening to recorded music.
Support their opinions and judgements about music by referring to objective observations.	In this Programme, pupils analyse and evaluate music they encounter. This informs their performing and composing and includes syncopation, tonality and a progressively extended pitch-range.

(S/C = Skill/Concept)

APPENDIX

'Growing with Music' in relation to
Music Curriculum and Assessment Policy in Scotland

PROGRAMME OF STUDY STRANDS	'GROWING WITH MUSIC'
Summary of Levels A – D:	**Observations and examples from the Programme:**
Investigating and exploring sound A Sounds in the environment. Contrasts of sound. B Exploring wider range of sounds and sound quality. C Mood in music. Obtaining subtle effects. D Experimenting. Electronic sound sources and computer programs. Simple acoustics.	The Programme is based upon a Skill/Concept index for which a sequence of skills, concepts and musical features have been carefully selected. These include features relating to mood, texture and expressiveness, encouraging their use in appropriate ways for the inventing activities of the pupils. Notations are used which primarily enable and support music thinking processes.
Using the voice A Acquiring a song repertoire. Pitching in vocal range. B Developing vocal control. Songs from many cultures. C Singing with greater expression. Beginning two-parts. D Wider range of styles. More complex work in parts. Improvements to the quality of vocal sound. Breathing.	The Programme is based upon use of the voice and associated aural development. It shows how children need to find their voices before they are seven if they are to grow in confidence and self-esteem. Internalised musical thinking is a natural consequence of using the voice as a medium of musical expression because the child makes the sound and controls the way it is used. The Programme is based upon a Song collection of 253 songs, all carefully chosen for their suitability for particular age-ranges.
Using instruments A Learning to manipulate and care for instruments. B Showing control of speed and dynamics. Techniques. C Playing by ear, from parts and with expression. D Practising more complex parts. Improving fluency and reaching higher levels of achievement.	A range of tuned and untuned instruments are recommended for use with this Programme. Instruments are first introduced not only to provide a range of sound textures, but mainly as an effective means of reinforcing acquired concepts. Instruments are used increasingly throughout the Programme to a point at which graded instrument ensemble material is achieved (scores and parts are provided as Copymasters). Graded choral music is also included in Copymaster form (Teacher's Book 2B).
Creating and designing A Inventing supported by the teacher. B Sound pictures. Recording and notation systems. C Short inventions to convey mood. Structure. D Composing, inventing and arranging. Structure. Inventing music for specific occasions.	The teaching programme in the Teacher's Book and the co-operative activities within the Pupil's Books regularly require pupils to respond to a variety of stimuli, including verse, stories, 'moods', specific occasions, drama and dance. Composing is a strong feature throughout and many opportunities to present performances of work done are suggested.
Communicating and presenting **A/B/C/D** Working co-operatively and showing respect for the opinions of others. Taking turns and accepting 'group responsibility'. Sharing performance with a variety of audiences and for a variety of occasions. Communicating with others through music whenever possible.	It is a constant feature that pupils work as a class, in groups and individually to perform with voice and instruments, and to analyse, evaluate and discuss musical ideas. The Pupil's Books, a valuable resource for Level B, frequently require the pupils to work in pairs, sharing tasks, taking turns and exchanging activities, so that essential communication and group responsibility takes place as a result.
Observing, listening, reflecting, describing and responding A Listening to sounds around. Stories/movement. B Short extracts. Expressing preferences. C Identifying genres. Discussing preferences. D Wide range of styles and genres. Live performance. Accepting criticism of musical structure and performance.	The Song collection and musical examples used in the Programme provides a rich repertoire of music from all continents of the world, including Scottish and Gaelic tradition. The Teacher's Book frequently gives background information about the material and its origins, as well as guidance on listening to recorded music. It also includes musical examples from different periods in European history.

276

'Growing with Music' in relation to National Curriculum Programmes of Study (Wales)

KEY
STAGE
2

PROGRAMME OF STUDY ITEM	'GROWING WITH MUSIC'
Pupils should:	**Observations and examples from the Programme:**
Memorise and internalise songs and musical ideas of increasing length and/or complexity.	The KS 2 Programme contains 155 songs in the Song collection, which are of increasing length and complexity.
Perform from simple notations and/or signals and understand a variety of musical instructions.	Based on performing and aural development, the pupils work with notations which enable extended musical thinking to take place, including staff notation and solfa pitch symbols/signs.
Sing an expanding repertoire of songs (unison and simple two-part), and pieces requiring a variety of vocal techniques, with increasing understanding and control of pitch, duration, dynamics, diction and phrasing.	The songs in KS 2 Song Collection are carefully chosen to be appropriate to the age of the pupils and the complexity of the work being undertaken: *the Teacher's Book has guidance on vocal technique, with vocal exercises.*
Perform pieces/accompaniments on a widening range of more sophisticated instruments, with increasing dexterity and control of sound.	At KS 2B, instruments are used increasingly – partly to reinforce and support acquired concepts, and partly to provide experience of playing in small ensembles: *S/C 6, 16, 22, 14, 39, orchestral file.*
Maintain a part as a member of a group in a simple part song.	Graded choral material in two parts is included in KS 2B. This draws upon British, European and world music.
Play an individual instrumental part in a group piece.	Graded instrumental ensemble material is included in KS 2B, with the opportunity to work from scores and parts.
Rehearse and direct performances.	An important feature of the Pupil's Books at KS 2 is that work with a partner or in groups is encouraged. This involves the constant use of techniques of negotiation and rehearsal.
Plan and present their own projects/performances, being aware of the need to communicate to different audiences.	The rich repertoire within the Programme provides an ideal basis for pupils to plan and present musical performances – most significantly because it is work prepared in class: *MUSIC IN OUR LIVES.*
Explore and use a widening range of sound sources.	This Programme uses vocal and instrumental sound sources. Other sound sources can readily be used as performing media, provided that they are appropriate to the work being undertaken.
Choose and arrange sounds to create a specific mood or atmosphere.	In KS 2B, there are many composing tasks in which pupils are asked to create music of appropriate mood for given situations, and to understand why particular effects are obtained.
Create music in response to a range of stimuli, using appropriate musical structures.	The Pupil's Books regularly ask pupils to respond to a range of stimuli, including verse, 'moods', specific occasions, drama, dance: *MUSIC IN OUR LIVES.* Composing is a strong feature throughout the Programme and there are opportunities to present performances.
Develop and refine musical ideas through improvising, composing and arranging.	The Programme requires pupils to work with music and develop ideas particularly through improvising and composing.
Communicate their ideas using recording equipment, signs and symbols, or cues.	Various forms of notation are used in the Programme and suggestions are made to the pupils from time to time about the value of recording their work.

'Growing with Music' in relation to
National Curriculum Programmes of Study (Wales)

KEY
STAGE
2

PROGRAMME OF STUDY ITEM	'GROWING WITH MUSIC'
Pupils should:	**Observations and examples from the Programme:**
Listen attentively and respond to music of different styles, times and cultures, and relate it to its historical and cultural background.	The repertoire contains music from all the continents of the world, and the Teacher's Book frequently gives background information about the material and its origins, as well as guidance on listening to recorded music.
Identify the characteristics of music from different styles and cultures.	The Programme addresses musical styles, including typical structural and expressive features, all of which are ingredients of the Programme's progressive structure: *S/C 24, 35, 44, 54, 58, 62, 64.*
Describe, discuss and undertake simple analysis and evaluation of music heard in class, including their own compositions and performances.	In this Programme, pupils analyse and evaluate music they encounter. This informs their performing and composing and includes syncopation, tonality and a progressively extended pitch-range.

(S/C = Skill/Concept)

Acknowledgements

Longman Group UK Limited
*Longman House, Burnt Mill, Harlow, Essex CM20 2JE, England
and Associated Companies throughout the World.*

© Longman Group UK Limited 1992

First published 1992
ISBN 0 582 03943 6
Set in 10½/12½ pt Rockwell Light (Linotron)

Printed and bound in Great Britain by
Butler & Tanner Ltd, Frome and London

The publisher's policy is to use paper manufactured
from sustainable forests.

Acknowledgements

We are grateful to the following for permission to reproduce
copyright material:

Association of Irish Choirs for the song 'Brian O'Linn' from *Read and
Sing* edited by Susan O'Regan; Cambridge University Press for the
songs 'Ao onipa dasani' and 'Raghupati' (translated by June Tillman) in
Light the Candles! (1991); Diogenes Verlag AG for the song 'Trarira,
der Sommer, der ist da' from *Das kleine Kinderliederbuch.* Copyright
© 1975 by Diogenes Verlag AG, Zurich. All rights reserved;
Scholastic Publications Ltd for 'The Ugsome Thing' by Ruth Ainsworth
from *The Ten Tales of Shellover*; Ward Lock Educational Company
Ltd for the songs 'Old Apple Tree we'll Wassail Thee' and 'Planting
Rice is Never Fun' in *A Musical Calendar of Festivals* by the late
Barbara Cass-Beggs and 'Now the Holly Bears the Berry' in *Brown
Bread and Butter* by Alison McMorland; Welsh Folk Song Society for
'Di didl lan dan dwdl didl' in *Canu'r Cymry II.*

Designed by Mick Harris
Illustrated by Paul Howard, Mandy Doyle and Kathy Baxandale
Cover illustration by Ian Newsham
Edited by Stephen Attmore